The MAILBOX®
The Education Center®

grades
PreK-1

Arts & Crafts
for Favorite THEMES

Over 250 all-new art activities!

- **Organized by teaching theme**
- **Makes use of everyday art materials**
- **Includes fun and creative art techniques**
- **Encourages student creativity**

Managing Editors: Kimberly Brugger-Murphy and Brenda Miner

Editorial Team: Becky S. Andrews, Randi Austin, Diane Badden, June Bass, Sarah Booth, Janet Boyce, Elizabeth Brandel, Amy Brinton, Joanne Brown, Tricia Brown, Kimberley Bruck, Karen A. Brudnak, Ann Bruehler, Gilda Cayne, Elizabeth Cook, Pam Crane, Kathryn Davenport, Roxanne LaBell Dearman, Shanda Fitte, Sue Fleischmann, Sarah Foreman, Pierce Foster, Deborah Garmon, Ada Goren, Heather Graley, Karen Guess, Shere R. Hallila, Tazmen Hansen, Marsha Heim, Lori Z. Henry, Lucia Kemp Henry, Kim Hintze, Linda Honold, Laura Johnson, Debra Kelley, Debra Liverman, Kitty Lowrance, Robin McClay, Amanda Monday, Jennifer Nunn, Nancy O'Toole, Tina Petersen, Robin Peterson, Diane Postman, Mark Rainey, Greg D. Rieves, Kelly Robertson, Hope Rodgers, Donna K. Teal, Babette Torres, Rachael Traylor, Sharon M. Tresino, Rachel G. Trevino, Christine Vohs, Brenda Watkins, Carole Watkins, Virginia Zeletzki

Projects on 40 popular teaching themes!

www.themailbox.com

HPS251390

Table of Contents

Fall Themes

Winter Themes

Spring and Summer Themes

Anytime Themes

Patterns

Personal Portrait

Materials for one:
tagboard picture frame
paper
assorted craft materials, such as foam shapes,
   pom-poms, feathers, and sequins
crayons, including flesh tones
glue

Steps:
1. Draw a self-portrait on the paper.
2. Glue the portrait facedown to the frame.
3. Turn the frame over and decorate it with
   desired craft items.

Glitter Crayons

Materials for one:
thin, colorful construction paper rectangles
construction paper
small paintbrush
crayons
glitter
glue

Steps:
1. Randomly glue rectangles to the paper.
2. Draw a triangle on one end of each rectangle
   using a crayon of a matching color.
3. Use the paintbrush to dab glue on each
   triangle; then sprinkle glitter of a matching
   color on the glue.

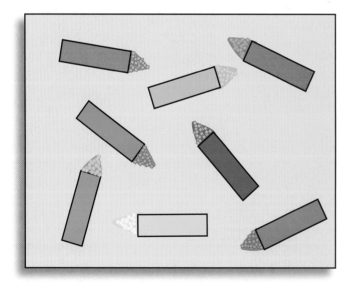

Jazzy Journal

Materials for one:
2 or more round kitchen scrubbers
12" x 18" construction paper
several sheets of writing paper
2 or more shallow containers of paint
3 paper fasteners
marker

Steps:
1. Dip a scrubber in paint and then press or whisk it on the paper.
2. Repeat the process with other scrubbers and colors of paint. Let the paint dry.
3. Fold the paper in half; then place the writing paper inside the folded paper. Secure the journal with the paper fasteners (with help as needed).
4. Write your name on the journal.

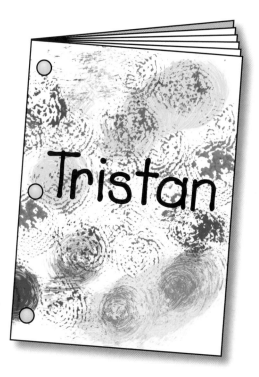

Shiny Yellow Bus

Materials for one:
2 black construction paper circles (wheels)
white construction paper school bus with windows
yellow tissue paper scraps
slightly diluted glue
crayons
paintbrush

Steps:
1. Draw a face in each window.
2. Brush glue on part of the bus; then press tissue paper on the glue.
3. Repeat the process until the bus is covered with tissue paper; then brush a layer of glue over the tissue paper.
4. Glue the wheels to the bus. After the glue is dry, trim any excess paper from the edge (with help as needed).

Fall

5

Hungry Worms

Materials for one:
9" x 12" red construction paper, trimmed into an
    apple shape
three 1¼" x 12" green construction paper worms
brown and green construction paper scraps
scissors
crayon
glue

Steps:
1. Fold the apple in half horizontally.
2. Starting at the fold, cut several slits, stopping each
   slit before reaching the edge. Unfold the apple.
3. Weave a worm through the slits. Weave the
   remaining worms, alternating the pattern with each
   worm added.
4. Draw a face on each worm.
5. Cut a stem and leaves from the paper scraps and
   glue them to the apple.

Sweet Apple Pie

Materials for one:

cinnamon-sugar in a shaker	6" disposable bowl
aluminum foil	light brown paint
six ½" x 6" brown construction	paintbrush
paper strips	glue
brown tissue paper scraps	scissors
6" paper plate	stapler

Steps:
1. Paint the back of the plate; then sprinkle cinnamon-sugar
   on the wet paint. Shake off the excess.
2. Glue the strips to the plate in a crisscross pattern. Trim
   any excess paper.
3. Wrap the bowl with aluminum foil so it resembles a small
   pie tin.
4. Staple the plate to the bowl.
5. Glue crumpled tissue paper around the edge of the plate
   so it resembles the edge of a piecrust.

Basketful of Apples

Materials for one:

sheet of plastic canvas
5" x 8" piece of a paper
    lunch bag
9" x 12" construction paper
green construction paper
    scraps

5" red, green, and yellow
    tissue paper squares
tape
brown unwrapped crayon
scissors
shallow container of glue

Setup:
   Draw a simple basket outline on the lunch bag paper. Tape the canvas to a table. Then lightly tape the paper to the canvas.

Steps:
   1. Rub the side of the brown crayon on the basket to give the basket a textured look.
   2. Cut out the basket and then glue it to the bottom of the paper.
   3. Crumple a tissue paper square, dip it in the glue, and then press it on the paper above the basket. Repeat the process to "fill" the basket with apples.
   4. Cut leaves from the construction paper scraps and glue them to the apples.

Lovely Apple Tree

Materials for one:

brown construction paper tree
9" x 12" construction paper
green construction paper scraps
round printing items, such as a film canister with its
    cap, a cylinder-shaped block, or a circular sponge
shallow containers of red, green, and yellow paint
brown and green crayons
scissors
glue

Steps:
   1. Glue the tree to the paper.
   2. Cut or tear leaves from the green construction paper scraps and glue them to the tree.
   3. To make an apple, dip a printing item in paint and press it on the paper.
   4. Repeat the process with other items and colors of paint.
   5. When the paint is dry, draw stems and leaves on the apples.

Fall

Apple Magnet

Materials for one:
self-adhesive magnetic strip
tagboard apple (no stem or leaves)
small green construction paper worm
brown and green construction paper scraps
red, green, or yellow tissue paper scraps
slightly diluted glue
paintbrush
crayon
scissors

Steps:
1. Brush a layer of glue on the apple.
2. Tear tissue paper scraps and press them on the glue.
3. Draw a face on the worm; then glue the worm to the apple.
4. Cut a stem and leaves from the paper scraps and glue them to the apple.
5. Brush a layer of glue over the apple.
6. After the glue is dry, trim any excess paper from around the edge; then attach the magnet.

Dotted Apples

Materials for one:
construction paper bowl shape
9" x 12" white construction paper
9" x 12" construction paper
red, green, and yellow stamp pads
unsharpened pencil for each stamp pad
brown and green markers
scissors
glue

Setup:
Draw several apple outlines (no stems or leaves) on the white construction paper.

Steps:
1. Press a pencil eraser on a stamp pad and then on an apple.
2. Repeat the process to fill each apple with eraser prints.
3. Glue the bowl to the construction paper.
4. Cut out the apples and glue them to the paper above the bowl.
5. Draw a stem and leaves on each apple.

Fall

Tubular Tree

Materials for one:

toilet paper tube
5" green construction paper square
2" fall-colored tissue paper squares
7 brown pipe cleaner halves

scissors
brown paint
paintbrush
glue

Setup:

In the top portion of the tube, use the point of the scissors to make six holes large enough for the pipe cleaners to slide through.

Steps:

1. Paint the tube brown; then glue one end to the construction paper square (ground). Let the paint and glue dry.
2. Glue crumpled tissue paper squares (leaves) to half of each pipe cleaner.
3. Slide a pipe cleaner into each hole and in the center of the tube.
4. Glue a few leaves to the ground.

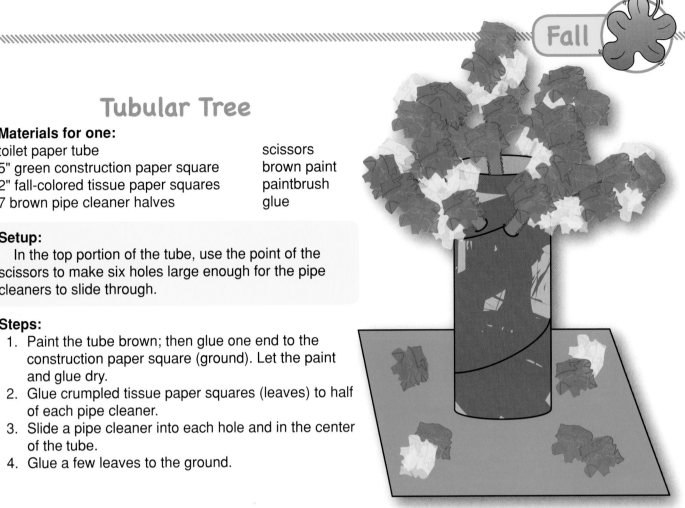

Fingerprint Squirrels

Materials for one:

9" x 12" construction paper
brown mini pom-poms (acorns)
shallow container of brown paint

crayons
black marker
glue

Steps:

1. Use the crayons to draw an outdoor scene that includes grass and a tree with autumn leaves.
2. Dip your index finger in the paint and then press it on the paper to make a squirrel head. Repeat the process using your thumb for the tail and your pinkie finger for the ears and paws. Make several squirrels.
3. When the paint has dried, draw facial details on each squirrel.
4. Glue an acorn between the paws of each squirrel.

Fall

Beautiful Foliage

Materials for one:
white construction paper
green and fall-colored tissue paper scraps
brown crayon
glue

Steps:
1. To make a tree, trace your forearm and hand on the white paper; then color the tree.
2. Tear the fall-colored tissue paper scraps and glue the pieces on the tree so they resemble leaves.
3. Glue torn green tissue paper scraps and a few colorful scraps on the bottom of the paper so they resemble grass and fallen leaves.

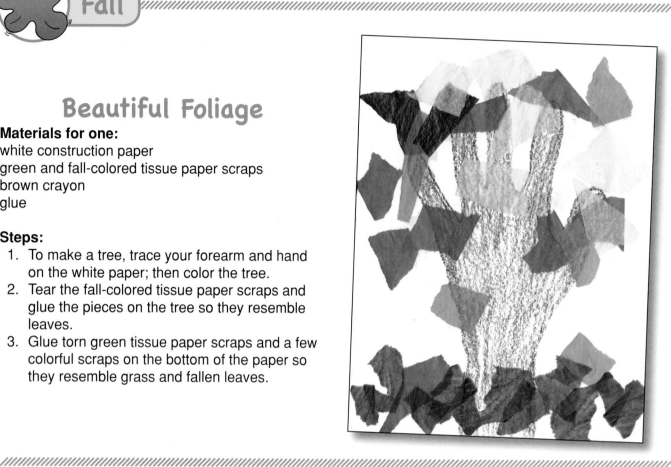

Amazing Acorn

Materials for one:
brown construction paper copy of page 131
chocolate candy sprinkles
shallow container of maple syrup
scissors
paintbrushes
glue

Steps:
1. Cut out the acorn.
2. Brush a layer of glue on the acorn cap.
3. Sprinkle candy sprinkles on the wet glue.
4. Paint the bottom of the acorn with the syrup.

Leafy Transfer

Materials for one:
several leaves (real or silk)
manila paper (or light-colored construction paper)
tray
shallow containers of fall-colored paint
sponge for each paint color
tape

Setup:
Put rolled tape on each leaf and then tape the leaves to the tray.

Steps:
1. Sponge-paint each leaf, overlapping the colors if you like.
2. Place the paper on top of the leaves and then gently rub your hand across the paper.
3. Lift the paper to reveal the leaf prints.

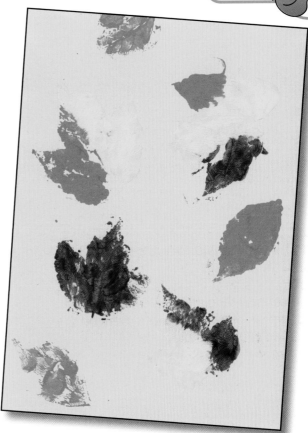

Loopy Leaves

Materials for one:
cardboard tube (tree trunk)   brown paint
colorful O-shaped cereal   scissors
colorful paper plate   paintbrush
lump of brown play dough   glue

Setup:
Cut a treetop shape from the paper plate. Cut two small slits opposite each other in one end of the tree trunk.

Steps:
1. Glue cereal to the treetop. Let the glue dry.
2. Paint the tree trunk and then press it into the play dough.
3. Slide the treetop in the slits in the trunk.

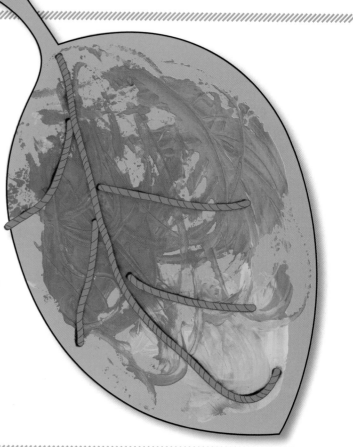

Autumn Colors

Materials for one:
large green construction paper leaf
jumbo craft stick
brown yarn
fall-colored paints
scissors

Steps:

1. Put small dollops of different-colored paints on the leaf.
2. Using the side of the craft stick, drag the paint across the leaf to create a colorful blend.
3. Cut pieces of yarn and press them on the wet paint so they resemble leaf veins.

Eye-Catching Mobile

Materials for one:
twig
several golf balls
construction paper leaves
large plastic tub (or box)
thin twine or yarn
plastic spoons
tape
shallow containers of fall-colored paint

Steps:

1. Lightly tape several leaves in the bottom of the tub.
2. Dip a golf ball in paint and then use a spoon to place it in the tub.
3. Tilt the tub to move the ball across the leaves, adding more paint to the ball as needed. Repeat with other balls and colors of paint. Let the paint dry.
4. Tape a length of twine to each leaf; then tie the loose end of the twine to the twig. Tie a length of twine to the twig (with help as needed) to make a hanger.

Stem Stamping

Materials for one:
chunky pumpkin stems
manila paper
shallow containers of fall-colored paint

Steps:
1. Dip a stem in paint and then press it on the paper.
2. Repeat the process with other stems and colors of paint.
3. Continue until the paper is filled with colorful prints, overlapping the colors if desired.

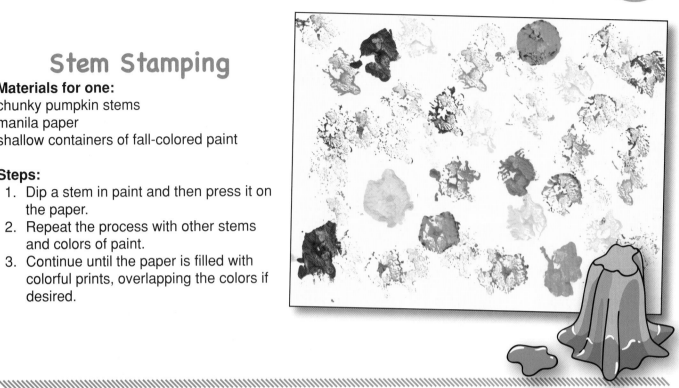

Autumn Wreath

Materials for one:
stem-stamped paper (see above idea)
small pinecones (optional)
bow or ribbon
large paper plate with the center removed
craft foam or construction paper acorns
chenille stem
scissors
glue
masking tape

Setup:
Cut leaf shapes from the stamped paper.

Steps:
1. Glue the leaves to the plate to make a wreath.
2. Glue pinecones and acorns to the wreath.
3. Glue the bow to the wreath. Let the glue dry.
4. To make a hanger, bend the chenille stem in half and tape it to the back of the wreath.

Wild-Haired Monster

Materials for one:
red paper rectangle
2 paper eyes
white foam cup (body)
pipe cleaner halves
crayons
scissors
glue

Steps:
1. Color the monster's body.
2. Cut a mouth from the red rectangle. Glue the mouth and eyes to the monster.
3. Twist the pipe cleaners and poke them into the top of the cup so they resemble hair.

Handy Owl

Materials for one:
2 small muffin liners
small orange triangle (beak)
9" x 12" brown construction paper
brown paper lunch bag
crayons
glue
scissors

Steps:
1. To make eyes, color the center of each muffin liner. Then glue the eyes to the bottom flap of the paper bag.
2. Glue the beak below the eyes.
3. Trace your hands on the construction paper and then cut out the tracings.
4. Glue the hand cutouts to the back of the owl so they look like wings.

A Home for Spider

Materials for one:
9" x 12" orange construction paper
large black pom-pom
four 4" lengths of black yarn
various lengths of white yarn
glue
scissors

Steps:
1. Draw a spiderweb on the paper.
2. Glue lengths of white yarn atop the drawing, cutting the yarn to fit as needed.
3. To make a spider, glue the black yarn to the pom-pom as shown.
4. Glue the spider to the web.

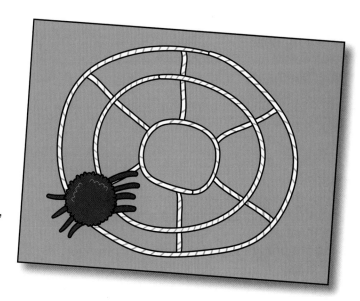

Squeeze a Web

Materials for one:
9" x 12" white construction paper
black paint
squeeze bottle of glue
black ink pad with washable ink
fine-tip black marker

Setup:
Mix several drops of black paint in the glue.

Steps:
1. Squeeze the glue mixture on the white paper so it resembles a spiderweb.
2. When the web is dry, press your fingertip on the ink pad and make several prints in and around the web.
3. Use the black marker to add details to the fingerprints so they look like spiders.

Color-Changing Jack-o'-Lantern

Materials for one:
pumpkin cutout slightly larger than a small
    paper plate
small paper plate
brad
crayons
scissors

Steps:

1. Color the paper plate using a variety of colors.
2. Draw eyes and a mouth on the pumpkin and cut them out.
3. Use the brad to attach the jack-o'-lantern to the plate.
4. Turn the plate to change the colors of the jack-o'-lantern's eyes and mouth.

Hanging Bat

Materials for one:

cardboard tube	paintbrush
9" x 12" black construction paper	hole puncher
2 paper eyes	white crayon
two 2" lengths of black pipe cleaner	scissors
black paint	glue

Steps:

1. To make the bat's body, paint the cardboard tube and let it dry.
2. Glue the eyes on the body.
3. Use the white crayon to trace your hands on the paper and then cut out the tracings (wings).
4. Glue the wings to the back and front of the body as shown.
5. Punch two holes near the bottom of the bat's body.
6. Insert a pipe cleaner in each hole and twist the pipe cleaner. Then bend the pipe cleaners so they resemble claws.
7. Hang the bat upside down by its claws.

Fall

Glimmering Ghosts

Materials for one:
9" x 12" black construction paper
salt
glue
paintbrush

Steps:
1. Paint glue in ghost shapes on the black paper.
2. Sprinkle salt on the glue.
3. Set the paper aside to dry.

Candy Corn Suncatcher

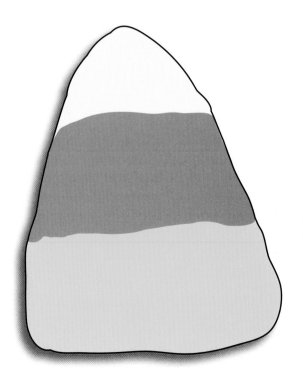

Materials for one:
X-Acto knife (for teacher use)
tagboard
waxed paper
orange and yellow paint
craft sticks
3 squeeze bottles of glue
tape

Setup:
To make a stencil, use the X-Acto knife to cut a large candy corn shape from the center of the tagboard. Mix several drops of orange paint in one bottle of glue and several drops of yellow paint in another.

Steps:
1. Tape the stencil atop the waxed paper.
2. Squirt a large blob of each color of glue within the stencil. Use craft sticks to spread the glue in rows so it looks like candy corn.
3. Remove the stencil and let the glue dry.
4. Peel off the waxed paper.

Sunny Sunflower

Materials for one:

coffee filter
yellow food coloring
cotton swab

shallow container of water
brown paint
scissors

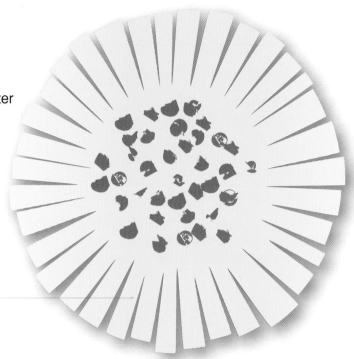

Setup:
Add several drops of yellow food coloring to the water.

Steps:
1. Place the coffee filter in the water; when the filter turns yellow, remove it and squeeze out the excess water.
2. When the coffee filter is dry, cut slits around the edge to make sections that resemble petals.
3. Dip the cotton swab in the paint and press it on the center of the coffee filter to make seeds. Repeat several times.

Flying Crow

Materials for one:

feather
paper plate
black, orange, and
   yellow paint

length of yarn
scissors
paintbrush
hole puncher

Setup:
Cut the plate in half. Set one half of the plate (body) so the straight edge is at the top. Cut a 1¼" slit as shown. To make wings, cut a 1¼" strip from the remaining plate half.

Steps:
1. Use the feather and black paint to paint both sides of the body and wings.
2. When the paint is dry, slide the wings through the slit.
3. Use the yellow paint to add eyes and the orange paint to add a beak.
4. Punch a hole near the top of the plate half. Thread the yarn through the hole and tie it to make a hanger.

body with slit

wings

Pumpkin Suncatcher

Materials for one:

sheet of waxed paper
1" squares of orange and yellow
   tissue paper
permanent marker
diluted glue

length of yarn
paintbrush
scissors
hole puncher

Setup:

   Use the permanent marker to draw a pumpkin on the waxed paper.

Steps:

1. Brush diluted glue on the waxed paper to cover the pumpkin.
2. Press tissue paper squares on the glue, making sure to overlap the orange and yellow pieces as much as possible.
3. When a desired effect is achieved, brush another layer of diluted glue over the tissue paper squares.
4. When the glue is dry, cut out the pumpkin. Punch a hole near the top of the pumpkin; then thread the yarn through the hole and tie it to make a hanger.

Pop-Up Pumpkin Patch

Materials for one:

four 3" pumpkin cutouts
four 1" x 3" paper strips
9" x 12" brown construction paper
   (pumpkin patch)
green yarn
glue
scissors

Steps:

1. Glue one end of a paper strip to the bottom of each pumpkin.
2. Fold each paper strip to make a tab.
3. Glue each tab to the pumpkin patch.
4. Cut a length of green yarn and glue it to the stem of each pumpkin so it looks like a vine.

Fresh-Picked Headband

Materials for one:

fall fruits and vegetables—such as apples, carrots, and potatoes—cut in half

3" x 18" strip of construction paper

shallow containers of paint

stapler

Setup:

Place two or three different produce halves near each paint color.

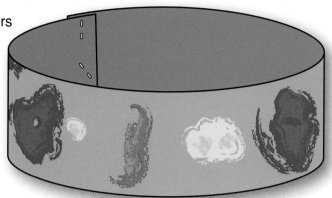

Steps:

1. Dip the cut side of a fruit or vegetable in a container of paint.
2. Gently press the fruit or vegetable on the paper strip to make a print.
3. Repeat Steps 1 and 2 using different fruits and vegetables and different colors of paint. When the paint is dry, staple the paper strip (with help as needed) to fit your head.

Colorful Corn

Materials for one:

green curling ribbon

3 white construction paper corncobs

cotton swabs

shallow containers of red, orange, yellow, and brown paint

hole puncher

scissors

glue

Setup:

Place two or more cotton swabs near each container of paint.

Steps:

1. Dip a cotton swab in a container of paint and press it on a corncob.
2. Repeat Step 1 with different colors of paint and corncobs.
3. Punch a hole in the larger end of each corncob.
4. Cut a length of curling ribbon and lace it through the holes in the corncob. Tie the ribbon and use scissors to curl the ends (with help as needed).
5. Glue the corncobs together as shown.

Harvest Candleholder

Materials for one:

small votive candle
small plastic
   margarine tub

dried corn and beans
plastic spoon
glue

Steps:
1. Pour beans and corn in the tub.
2. Mix in a generous amount of glue to coat the beans and corn.
3. Use the spoon to press the mixture to form a compacted layer.
4. Push the candle in the center of the mixture until only about a half inch is visible.
5. When the mixture is dry, pop the resulting candleholder out of the tub.

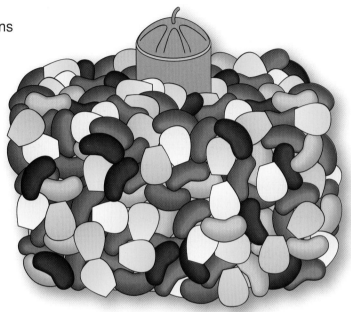

Roll the Gourds

Materials for one:

seasonal gourds
cardboard box, such as a shoebox
sheet of construction paper cut to fit inside the box
plastic spoons
paint

Steps:
1. Put the paper in the box.
2. Pour spoonfuls of paint on the paper.
3. Place one or more gourds in the box.
4. Gently tilt the box to roll the gourds through the paint.
5. When a desired effect is achieved, remove the gourds and set the paper aside to dry.

The Mayflower

Materials for one:

3" white paper square
paper plate
craft stick
brown crayon

scissors
black marker
glue

Steps:

1. Color the back of the paper plate brown.
2. Fold the plate in half and cut away a small section, as shown, to make a boat.
3. Use the black marker to write "The <u>Mayflower</u>" on the side of the boat.
4. Cut a sail from the white paper and glue it to one end of the craft stick. Glue the other end of the stick to the boat.

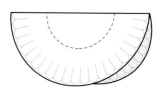

Little Pilgrims

Materials for one:

paper scraps
paper plate
scissors

crayons
glue

Steps:

1. Cut the plate as shown.
2. Draw a face in the center of the plate.
3. Color the bow.
4. To make a male pilgrim, color the area around the face so it resembles hair. Then make a hat from paper scraps and glue it to the pilgrim. To make a female pilgrim, cut paper scraps and glue them to the plate so they resemble hair behind a bonnet.

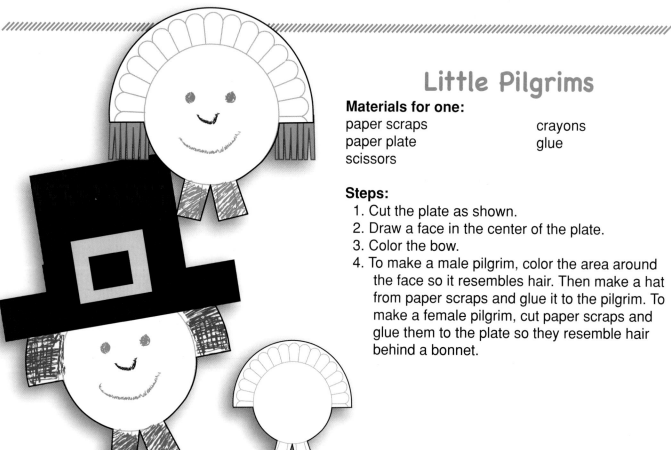

A Pilgrim's Hat

Materials for one:

small paper cup
black paper circle larger than
   the opening of the cup
yellow paper square

black paint
paintbrush
glue
scissors

Steps:

1. Paint the outside of the cup and let it dry.
2. Glue the circle to the opening of the cup.
3. Cut a buckle from the paper square and glue it to the cup.

Turkey Treat Holder

Materials for one:

brown paper turkey body
paper scraps
brown paper lunch bag
scissors
glue

Steps:

1. Cut off the top portion of the bag.
2. Glue the turkey body to the side of the bag without the flap. Then use the paper scraps to add details, such as eyes, a beak, and a wattle.
3. Cut from the paper scraps several turkey feathers. Then open the bag and glue the feathers to the bag opposite the turkey's body.

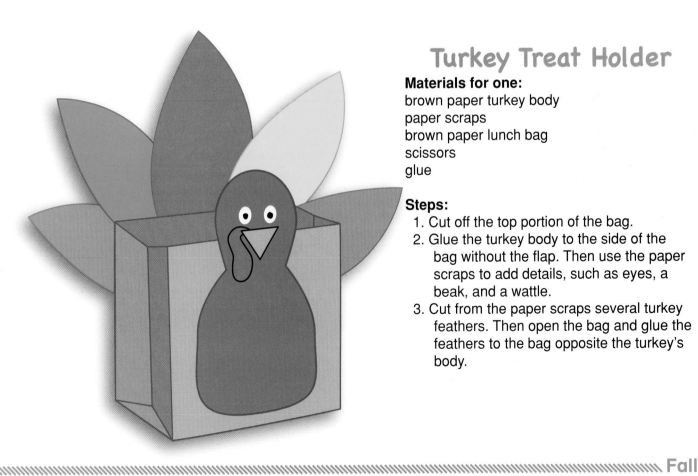

Fall

Thankful Banner

Materials for one:

9" construction paper square
used magazines
paint in several colors
sponges
yarn

black marker
hole puncher
glue
scissors

Steps:

1. Sponge-paint the paper square and allow it to dry.
2. Use the black marker to write your name on the square.
3. Cut out pictures that represent things for which you are thankful. Glue the pictures to the square.
4. Punch holes in the top corners of the square. Thread a piece of yarn through each hole to attach it to another square to create a banner display.

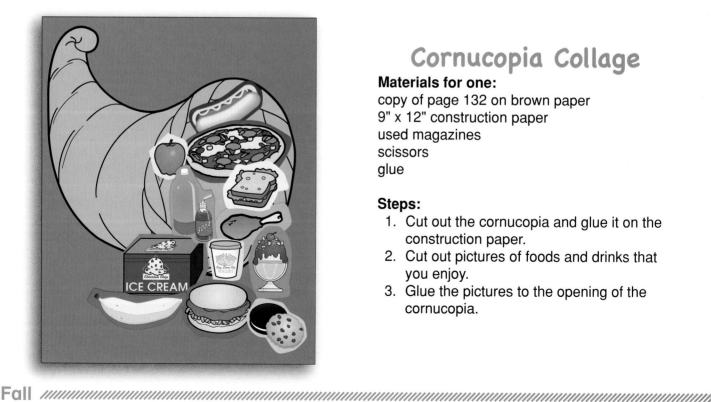

Cornucopia Collage

Materials for one:

copy of page 132 on brown paper
9" x 12" construction paper
used magazines
scissors
glue

Steps:

1. Cut out the cornucopia and glue it on the construction paper.
2. Cut out pictures of foods and drinks that you enjoy.
3. Glue the pictures to the opening of the cornucopia.

Icicles on the Roof

Materials for one:
construction paper
bulletin board border scraps
white paper scraps
scissors
glue
markers

Setup:
Cut one side of the construction paper so it resembles a rooftop. Then cut two border scraps to match the edges.

Steps:
1. Tear the paper scraps so they resemble icicles.
2. Glue the icicles to the back of a border; then glue the border to the construction paper.
3. Repeat the process with the remaining border.
4. Use markers to draw details, such as a door and windows, on the house.

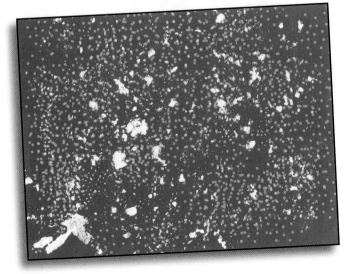

A Glistening Snowfall

Materials for one:
small porcupine ball
construction paper
container large enough to hold the paper
spoon
white paint
clear glitter

Steps:
1. Put the paper in the container.
2. Dip the ball in the paint and then use the spoon to place it on the paper.
3. Tilt the container back and forth, adding more paint to the ball as needed.
4. Sprinkle glitter on the wet paint.

A Wintry Scene

Materials for one:
construction paper
white hole reinforcers
crayons

Steps:
1. Draw an outdoor scene on the paper.
2. Attach hole reinforcers so they resemble snowflakes.

Fuzzy Mitten

Materials for one:
latch-hook yarn
construction paper mitten

scissors
paintbrush
glue

Steps:
1. Brush a thick layer of glue on part of the mitten.
2. Hold a small bundle of yarn above the mitten; then cut tiny pieces of yarn off the end of the bundle so the scraps fall on the glue.
3. Repeat until the mitten is covered with a layer of yarn scraps.

Hot Chocolate

Materials for one:
chocolate syrup
tagboard mug
seasonal stickers
white mini pom-poms (marshmallows)
paintbrush

Steps:
1. Paint the top of the mug with the chocolate syrup.
2. Press marshmallows in the syrup.
3. Use the stickers to decorate the mug.

Pouf Snowpal

Materials for one:
pouf mesh sponges (small, medium, and large)
construction paper
construction paper scraps
assorted craft materials, such as fabric scraps, small twigs, yarn, and ribbon
shallow container of white paint
hole puncher
scissors
glue

Steps:
1. Dip each sponge in the paint and press it on the paper to make a snowpal.
2. Use craft materials, paper scraps, the hole puncher, and scissors to make snowpal details, such as eyes, a nose, a mouth, a scarf, and a hat.
3. Glue the items to the snowpal.

Snow Globe

Materials for one:

clear plastic wrap
2 paper plates
markers

squeeze bottle of glue
scissors

Setup:

Cut the center from one plate and save the cutout to use in Step 3. Cut a piece of plastic wrap larger than the hole in the plate.

Steps:

1. Squeeze glue around the hole on the front of the plate. Place the plastic wrap over the hole and press it on the glue. Let the glue dry.
2. Draw a wintry scene on the front center of the remaining plate.
3. Hold the circle cutout from the first plate above the wintry scene and cut or tear it into tiny pieces.
4. Glue the front side of the plate with the plastic wrap window atop the plate with the snow.

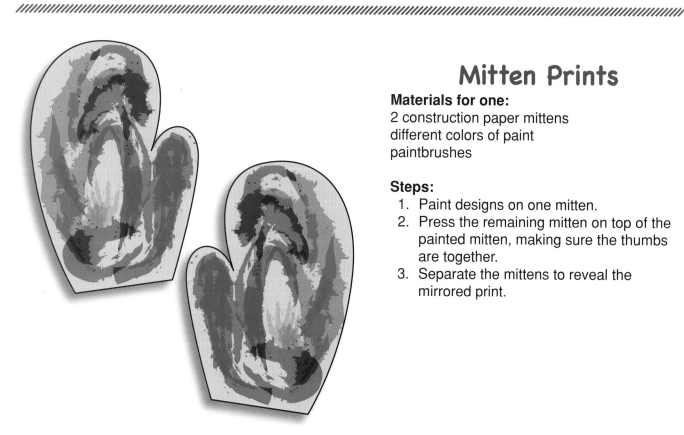

Mitten Prints

Materials for one:

2 construction paper mittens
different colors of paint
paintbrushes

Steps:

1. Paint designs on one mitten.
2. Press the remaining mitten on top of the painted mitten, making sure the thumbs are together.
3. Separate the mittens to reveal the mirrored print.

Arts & Crafts for Favorite Themes • ©The Mailbox® Books • TEC61262

Sparkling Snowflake

Materials for one:
piece of lace
white play dough mixed with glitter
6 cotton swabs

Steps:
1. Mold the play dough into a snowflake-like shape.
2. Press lace on the dough and remove it to create a textured design.
3. Push the cotton swabs into the dough to make the snowflake's points.

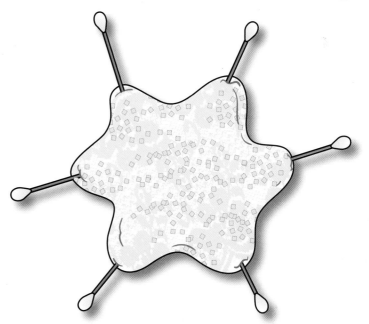

Adorable Snowpal

Materials for one:

white tube sock
cotton batting
condiment cup
assorted craft materials, such
   as fabric scraps, pom-poms,
   ribbon, and craft foam scraps

3 rubber bands
glue
paint (optional)
paintbrush (optional)

Steps:
1. Stuff the sock with cotton batting.
2. Wrap a rubber band around the opening of the sock to seal it.
3. Wrap a rubber band around the sock to make a head; then wrap another rubber band around the sock to make a stomach.
4. Use craft materials to make snowpal details, such as eyes, a nose, a mouth, a scarf, and a belt.
5. Glue the details to the snowpal. Glue the condiment cup to the snowpal's head, painting the cup first if desired.

Winter Wonderland

Materials for one:
Epsom salts mixed with water
construction paper
crayons
paintbrush

Steps:
1. Color a wintry scene on the paper.
2. Brush the salt solution over the picture.

Snowy Evergreen

Materials for one:

tagboard tree	paintbrush
flour	iridescent glitter
white paint	

Setup:
  Mix the flour and paint to achieve a desired consistency.

Steps:
1. Paint the tree with the mixture.
2. Shake glitter on the tree.

Snowball Fun

Materials for one:
nonmentholated shaving cream
large pom-pom
construction paper
clear or iridescent glitter
glue

Setup:
   Mix together equal amounts of shaving cream and glue.

Steps:
1. Dip the pom-pom in the shaving cream mixture and then mash it on the paper.
2. Repeat until you are satisfied with your work.
3. Sprinkle glitter on the wet mixture.

Snowpal's Snowstorm

Materials for one:
hairbrush
blue construction paper
construction paper scraps
cotton batting or cotton balls
assorted craft materials, such
   as craft foam scraps, fabric
   scraps, and yarn

shallow container of
   white paint
white crayon
scissors
glue

Steps:
1. Use the crayon to draw a snowpal outline on the paper.
2. Glue pieces of cotton batting to the snowpal.
3. Use the craft materials and paper scraps to make snowpal details—such as eyes, a nose, a mouth, and arms—and then glue them to the snowpal.
4. Dip the hairbrush in the paint and then tap it on the paper around the snowpal, adding more paint to the brush as needed.

Unique Snowflake

Materials for one:

golf ball
spoon
scissors
coffee filter

container such as a large shoebox
shallow container of paint
glitter

Steps:

1. Fold the filter several times and then cut out shapes around the edge.
2. Unfold the paper and place it in the container.
3. Dip the golf ball in the paint and then use the spoon to put it in the container.
4. Tilt the container back and forth to move the golf ball, adding more paint to the ball as needed.
5. Sprinkle glitter on the wet paint.

Sparkling Pinecone

Materials for one:

pinecone
Epsom salts or glitter
ribbon
shallow container of white paint

Setup:

Tie a length of ribbon to the top of the pinecone.

Steps:

1. Hold the ribbon and dip, drag, or swirl the pinecone in the paint.
2. Sprinkle salt or glitter on the pinecone and then hang it by the ribbon to dry.

Polar Bear Crossing

Materials for one:
copy of the polar bear pattern on page 133
construction paper
small block
length of white yarn
shallow container of white paint
scissors
tape

Steps:
1. Dip the block in the paint and press it on the paper. Repeat as many times as you wish, adding more paint to the block as needed. Let the paint dry.
2. Cut out the polar bear.
3. Tape one end of the yarn to the back of the bear and the other end to the back of the paper.

Perky Penguin

Materials for one:
baby wipes
large black construction paper oval (body)
black construction paper circle (head)
construction paper scraps, including black

2 hole reinforcers (eyes)
shallow container of white paint
glue
scissors

Setup:
Place the container of baby wipes nearby for cleanup.

Steps:
1. Remove a shoe and sock.
2. Dip your foot in the paint and then press it on the body. Use the wipes to clean your foot; then put on your sock and shoe.
3. Glue the head to the body; then attach the eyes to the head.
4. Cut or tear the black paper scraps to make wings and use other scraps to make a beak and feet; then glue the pieces to the body.

Arctic Hare

Materials for one:

toothbrush
fingerpaint paper
newsprint bunny
shallow containers of
    black and white paint

water
foam roller

Steps:

1. Moisten the bunny and smooth it onto the fingerpaint paper.
2. Roll a layer of black paint over the entire paper.
3. Remove the bunny.
4. Dip the toothbrush in the white paint and then run your finger across the bristles, splattering paint on the paper to make snow. Add more paint to the toothbrush as needed.

Snowy Owl

Materials for one:

cotton batting
white construction paper
    oval (body)
light blue construction paper
white and yellow construction
    paper scraps

white facial tissue
marker
glue
paintbrush
scissors

Steps:

1. Glue the body to the paper; then cut two wings from the white paper scraps and glue one to each side of the body.
2. Tear tissue into small pieces; then brush glue on part of the owl and press the pieces on the glue. Continue until the owl is covered with tissue; then use the marker to make spots on the owl.
3. Cut two eyes and a beak from the yellow paper scraps and glue them to the owl; then use the marker to draw details on the eyes.
4. Glue cotton batting to the bottom of the page so it looks like the owl is standing in snow.

Holiday Banner

Materials for one:

used holiday cards   stapler
sheet of felt   scissors
yarn or ribbon   glue
straw   glitter

Setup:

Tie a length of yarn or ribbon to the straw so it forms a hanger. Staple the hanger to one end of the felt as shown.

Steps:

1. Place the felt on a table with the hanger in the back.
2. Cut pictures from the cards and glue them to the felt.
3. Squeeze glue on spaces between the pictures; then sprinkle glitter on the glue.

Angel Rubbings

Materials for one:

2 heart-shaped doilies   unwrapped crayons
small construction paper   scissors
   circle (head)   glue
white copy paper

Setup:

To make an angel, cut a pair of wings from a doily. Attach the head, wings, and a second doily to a sheet of paper.

Steps:

1. Place a piece of paper on top of the angel.
2. Rub the side of a crayon on the paper over the angel.
3. Move the paper and repeat, using different-colored crayons and overlapping the rubbings.

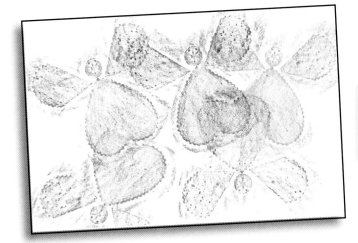

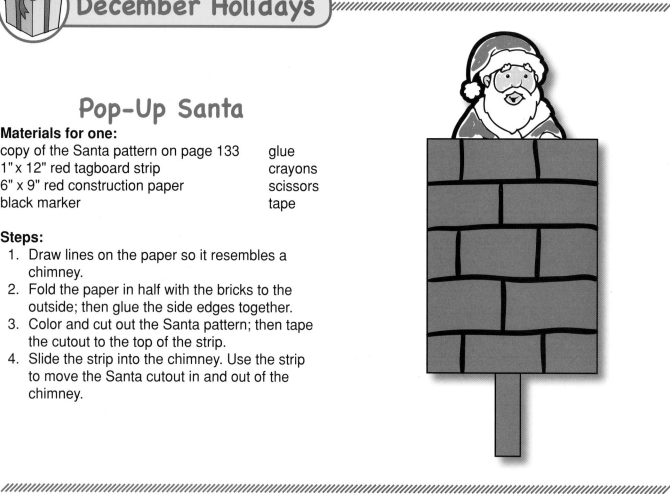

Pop-Up Santa

Materials for one:

copy of the Santa pattern on page 133   glue
1" x 12" red tagboard strip   crayons
6" x 9" red construction paper   scissors
black marker   tape

Steps:

1. Draw lines on the paper so it resembles a chimney.
2. Fold the paper in half with the bricks to the outside; then glue the side edges together.
3. Color and cut out the Santa pattern; then tape the cutout to the top of the strip.
4. Slide the strip into the chimney. Use the strip to move the Santa cutout in and out of the chimney.

Kwanzaa Placemat

Materials for one:

white construction paper
red, black, and green tissue paper strips
foam paintbrush
container of water

Steps:

1. Lay the strips on the paper in any pattern you like.
2. Paint each strip with water.
3. When the tissue paper is dry, remove it from the construction paper.

Ornamental Wreath

Materials for one:

headshot photo
small paper plate with
    center removed
green paper shreds
craft materials, such as
    pom-poms, sequins, and
    holiday-related shapes

2" piece of yarn
ribbon (optional)
paintbrush
glue
tape

Steps:

1. Brush glue on the front of the plate; then press paper shreds on the glue.
2. Glue craft materials to the shreds.
3. Tape one end of the yarn to the back of the photo and the other end to the back of the plate so the photo hangs in the center of the wreath.

Textured Tree

Materials for one:

nonmentholated shaving cream
tagboard tree
craft materials, such as pom-poms, sequins, strips
    of thin garland, and tinsel
glue
green paint

Setup:

    Mix equal amounts of shaving cream and glue; then tint the mixture with green paint.

Steps:

1. Use the mixture to fingerpaint the tree.
2. Press craft items onto the tree while the mixture is wet.

Winter

Shake, Rattle, and Paint

Materials for one:

cookie tin with lid
large jingle bell
construction paper cut into
   a holiday-related shape

plastic spoon
shallow container of paint
glitter

Steps:

1. Place the shape in the tin.
2. Dip the bell in the paint and then use the spoon to put it in the tin.
3. Put the lid on and then tilt and shake the tin to roll the bell.
4. Remove the lid and the bell; then shake glitter on the wet paint.

Star of David Ornament

Materials for one:

waxed paper
blue yarn
ribbon

scissors
container of diluted glue
gold glitter

Setup:

   Draw two triangles on a sheet of waxed paper to form a Star of David. Cut two lengths of yarn, each long enough to fit around one triangle.

Steps:

1. Dip the yarn in the glue to saturate it.
2. Pull the yarn between your fingers to remove the excess glue.
3. Place the yarn on a triangle outline. Repeat for the second triangle, overlapping the yarn on the first triangle.
4. Shake glitter on the yarn.
5. After the glue dries, gently peel the ornament from the waxed paper and attach the ribbon (with help as needed) for hanging.

Candy Cane Stripes

Materials for one:

peppermint extract (optional)   red and green paint
white tagboard candy cane   paintbrushes
masking tape   glitter

Setup:

If desired, add a few drops of peppermint extract to each color of paint.

Steps:

1. Press strips of masking tape on the candy cane to make stripes.
2. Paint the candy cane in any pattern you like.
3. Shake glitter on the wet paint.
4. When the paint is dry, gently remove the tape from the candy cane.

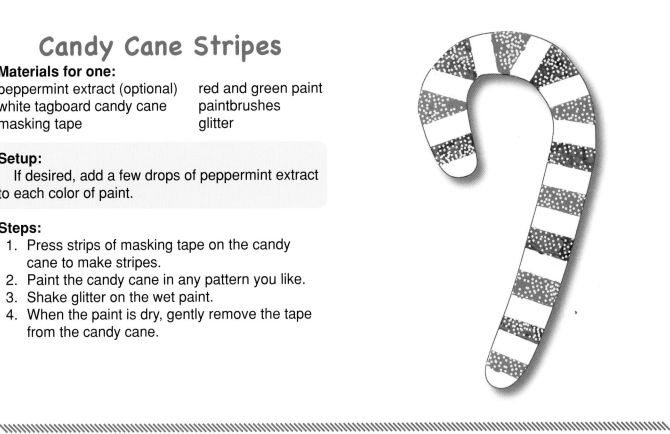

Cookie Cutter Creations

Materials for one:

cookie sheet   construction paper
aluminum foil   shallow containers
holiday-related   of paint
    cookie cutters   glitter

Steps:

1. Place a sheet of aluminum foil on the cookie sheet.
2. Press a cookie cutter in paint and then on the foil. Repeat.
3. Sprinkle glitter on the wet paint.
4. When the paint is dry, attach the foil to the construction paper.

Winter

Angelic Keepsake

Materials for one:

headshot photo
toilet paper tube
aluminum foil, sized to fit the tube
white construction paper
chenille glitter stem

glitter
tape
scissors
glue

Setup:

Shape one end of the chenille stem so it resembles a halo.

Steps:

1. Wrap the aluminum foil around the tube and tape it in place.
2. Tape the photo to one end of the tube; then tape the chenille stem to the back of the tube so the halo rests above the photo.
3. Trace your hands on the paper. Cut out the tracings (wings).
4. Spread glue on the wings and then sprinkle glitter on the glue.
5. Glue the wings to the tube.

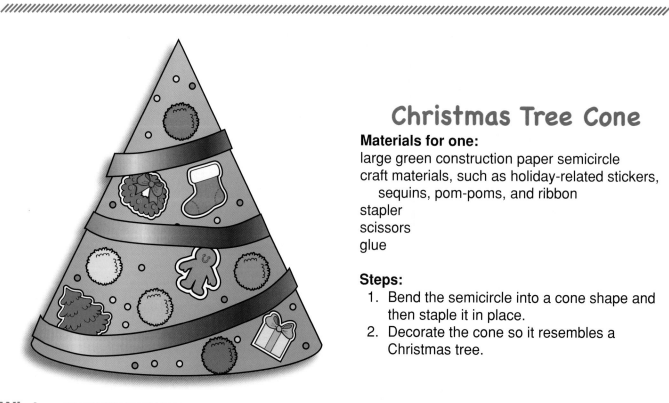

Christmas Tree Cone

Materials for one:

large green construction paper semicircle
craft materials, such as holiday-related stickers, sequins, pom-poms, and ribbon
stapler
scissors
glue

Steps:

1. Bend the semicircle into a cone shape and then staple it in place.
2. Decorate the cone so it resembles a Christmas tree.

Adorable Photo Ornament

Materials for one:

clear plastic ornament
piece of garland
headshot photo

ribbon
permanent marker

Steps:

1. Arrange the photo and garland in the ornament.
2. Tie the ribbon to the ornament to make a hanger.
3. Write your name and the date on the ornament.

Kwanzaa Shaker

Materials for one:

cardboard tube
uncooked rice
5" red, green, and black
   tissue paper squares
   (2 of each color)

red, green, and black
   tissue paper scraps
2 rubber bands
slightly diluted glue
paintbrush

Steps:

1. Brush glue on the tube; then press tissue paper scraps on the glue.
2. Cover one end of the tube with a layer of red, green, and black tissue paper squares; then secure them with a rubber band.
3. Pour a small amount of rice in the tube.
4. Cover the opening with the remaining squares and secure them with a rubber band.

Winter

Triangular Tree Puzzle

Materials for one:

die-cut star
brown rectangle (tree trunk)
9 equal-size construction
 paper triangles
construction paper
colorful sticky dots
glue

Setup:

Make a puzzle base on the construction paper as shown. Cut it out.

Steps:

1. Glue each triangle to a space on the base.
2. Glue the star to the top of the puzzle and the tree trunk to the bottom.
3. Peel sticky dots from their backing and press them on the tree.

Menorah Magnet

Materials for one:

self-adhesive magnetic strip
construction paper rectangle
eight ½" x 3" construction paper strips (candles)
one ½" x 4" construction paper strip (shamash)
jumbo craft stick
small yellow tissue paper scraps
craft materials, such as glitter pens and holiday-related
 shapes and stickers
glue

Steps:

1. Glue the candles to the craft stick, placing the shamash in the center.
2. Glue the rectangle to the bottom of the craft stick.
3. Glue crumpled tissue paper to each candle so it resembles a flame.
4. Decorate the menorah with the craft materials.
5. Peel the backing off the magnetic strip and press the strip on the back of the menorah.

Decoupage Candy Cane

Materials for one:

white construction paper
   candy cane
red, white, and green
   tissue paper scraps

slightly diluted glue
paintbrush
scissors

Steps:

1. Brush glue on part of the candy cane.
2. Tear tissue paper scraps and press them on the glue.
3. Repeat the process to decorate the candy cane.
4. Brush a layer of glue over the tissue paper.
5. When the glue is dry, trim any excess paper from the edge (with help as needed).

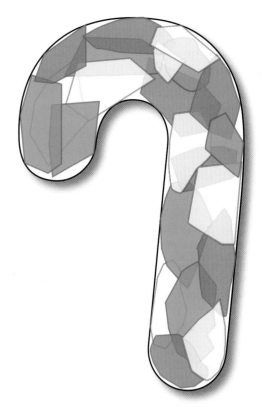

Merry Christmas

Decoupage Greeting Card

Materials for one:

2 decoupage candy
   canes (see above)
personal photo, trimmed
   into a heart shape

12" x 18" construction paper
glue
markers

Steps:

1. Fold the construction paper in half to make a card.
2. Glue the candy canes to the front of the card so they form a heart shape.
3. Glue the photo inside the heart.
4. Write (or dictate) a greeting and message.
5. Write your name inside the card.

Winter

Peaceful World

Materials for one:

people cutouts
white construction
   paper circle
tray

blue and green paint
small paintbrush
black marker
glue

Steps:

1. Put a generous amount of each paint on the tray.
2. Use the paintbrush to swirl the paint.
3. Place the circle on the paint and then gently rub your hand across the circle. Remove the circle and let the paint dry.
4. Write the words "Peaceful World" in the center of the circle.
5. Glue people cutouts around the edge of the circle.

I Have a Dream

Materials for one:

white construction paper cloud
3" skin-tone construction paper circle (head)
4½" construction paper pillow
twelve 2" colorful construction paper squares
9" x 12" construction paper
tissue paper scraps or small pieces of yarn (hair)
markers
glue

Setup:

Draw a line six inches from the bottom of the paper.

Steps:

1. To make the quilt, glue the squares below the line to make three rows of four squares.
2. Glue the pillow above the quilt; then glue the head to the pillow.
3. On the head, draw facial features with the eyes closed as if sleeping. Then glue hair to the head.
4. Dictate or write words on the cloud describing your dream for a happy world. Glue the cloud above the head.

Groundhog's Shadow

Materials for one:

2 white construction paper
   groundhogs (pattern on
   page 134)

brad fastener
black paint
brown crayon

Steps:

1. Fingerpaint a groundhog black so it
   resembles a shadow. Let the paint dry.
2. Color the remaining groundhog brown.
3. Place the brown groundhog atop its shadow
   and connect them at the feet with the brad.
4. Reveal the shadow by moving the black
   groundhog.

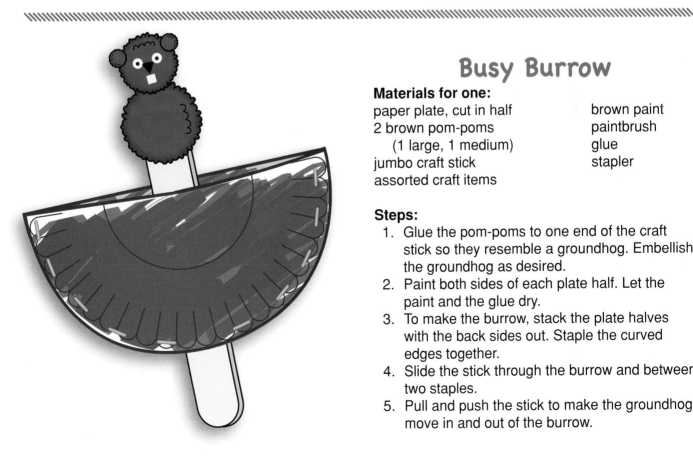

Busy Burrow

Materials for one:

paper plate, cut in half
2 brown pom-poms
   (1 large, 1 medium)
jumbo craft stick
assorted craft items

brown paint
paintbrush
glue
stapler

Steps:

1. Glue the pom-poms to one end of the craft
   stick so they resemble a groundhog. Embellish
   the groundhog as desired.
2. Paint both sides of each plate half. Let the
   paint and the glue dry.
3. To make the burrow, stack the plate halves
   with the back sides out. Staple the curved
   edges together.
4. Slide the stick through the burrow and between
   two staples.
5. Pull and push the stick to make the groundhog
   move in and out of the burrow.

Patriotic Banner

Materials for one:
5" x 12" blue construction paper
12" x 18" white construction paper
yarn
patriotic stickers, such as foil stars and flags
squeeze bottle of red paint
glue
hole puncher
scissors

Setup:
Trim one end of the white paper as shown. Fold the paper in half vertically.

Steps:
1. Unfold the white paper (banner) and squeeze lines of paint on one side.
2. Refold the banner and gently rub your hand across the surface. Then unfold the banner and let the paint dry.
3. Glue the blue paper to the top of the banner and decorate it with stickers.
4. Punch a hole in each upper corner of the banner. Tie a length of yarn to the holes to make a hanger.

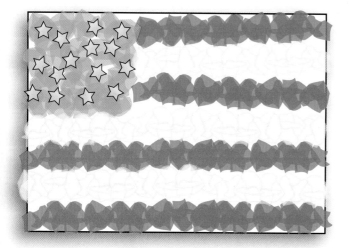

Sticky Flag

Materials for one:
American flag (optional)   red, white, and blue
clear Con-Tact   tissue paper scraps
   covering rectangle   foil star stickers

Setup:
Place the American flag nearby to use as a guide if desired.

Steps:
1. Peel the backing off the rectangle and place the rectangle on a table sticky-side up.
2. Tear tissue paper scraps and press them on the covering so they resemble the pattern of the American flag.
3. Peel star stickers from their backing and press them on the tissue.

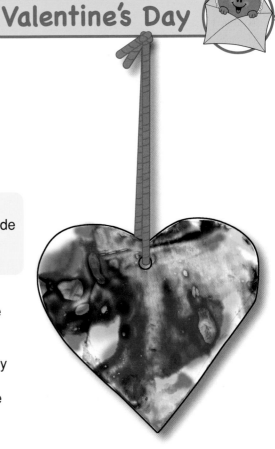

Suncatcher Heart

Materials for one:

two 8" clear Con-Tact
   covering squares
different colors of paint
plastic spoon for each
   paint color
yarn
scissors
hole puncher
permanent marker

Setup:

   Use a permanent marker to draw a large heart on the clear side of one square. Peel the backing off the square and place it on a table sticky-side up.

Steps:

1. Use the spoons to drizzle different colors of paint inside the heart.
2. Peel the backing off the second square and carefully place the square sticky-side down over the painted square. Gently rub your hand across the covering. Let the paint dry.
3. Cut out the heart shape; then punch a hole at the top of the heart and attach a length of yarn for hanging.

Heartfelt Sentiment

Materials for one:

large construction paper heart
two 1" x 12" paper strips
9" x 12" construction paper
markers
tape
scissors

Steps:

1. Draw a face on the heart.
2. Accordion-fold each strip; then tape one end of each strip to the back of the heart to make arms.
3. Trace your hands on the construction paper.
4. Cut out the tracings and tape each cutout to the end of a different arm.
5. Write "I love you" on one hand cutout and "this much!" on the other.

Winter

Puppy Cardholder

Materials for one:

empty pasta box
large construction paper
   heart (head)
2 medium construction
   paper hearts (ears)
small construction paper
   heart (nose)

sheet of construction paper cut
   to fit the box's width and height
construction paper scraps
glue
scissors
tape
black marker

Steps:

1. Arrange the head with the point facing upward; then glue the ears and nose to the head.
2. Cut two eyes and a tongue from paper scraps and glue them in place. Use the marker to draw details on the eyes and nose.
3. Wrap the paper around the box and tape it in place.
4. Glue the head to the box.
5. Cut a tail from a paper scrap and glue it to the back of the box.

Love Bug

Materials for one:

large white construction paper heart
large red construction paper
   heart cut in half (wings)
small red construction paper
   heart (head)
2 small thin black paper
   strips (antennae)
brad
red paint
paintbrush
black marker
tape

Steps:

1. Paint the palm and fingers of your hand; then press your hand on the white heart. Let the paint dry.
2. Draw spots on each wing and facial details on the head.
3. Tape the antennae to the back of the head.
4. Write (or have someone write for you) a special message on the white heart.
5. Slightly overlap the bottom of the wings and place them atop the white heart. Place the head atop the overlapped wings and connect the pieces with the brad.
6. Spread the wings to reveal the message.

Daddy,
I love you
so much!

Winter

Swirled Heart

Materials for one:
nonmentholated shaving cream
heart cut from 9" construction
    paper square
white paint
food coloring
paintbrush
craft stick

Setup:
    Mix equal amounts of white paint and shaving cream to make puff paint.

Steps:
1. Paint the heart with the puff paint.
2. Drip food coloring on the heart. Then use the craft stick to swirl the colors.

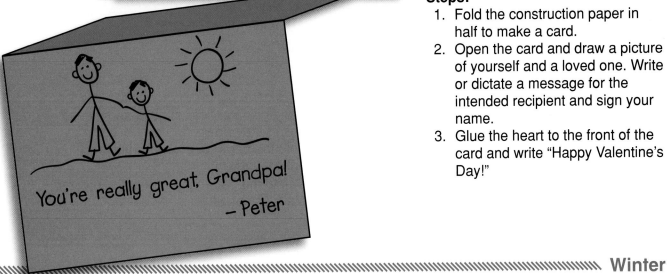

Happy Valentine's Day!

You're really great, Grandpa!
    – Peter

Valentine's Day Card

Materials for one:
swirled heart (See the idea above.)
12" x 18" construction paper
glue
markers

Steps:
1. Fold the construction paper in half to make a card.
2. Open the card and draw a picture of yourself and a loved one. Write or dictate a message for the intended recipient and sign your name.
3. Glue the heart to the front of the card and write "Happy Valentine's Day!"

Winter

Dental Health Mobile

Materials for one:

white construction paper teeth
3" x 18" tagboard strip
　(toothbrush handle)
large blank index card
magazine with pictures of
　healthy foods

dental floss
scissors
tape
glue

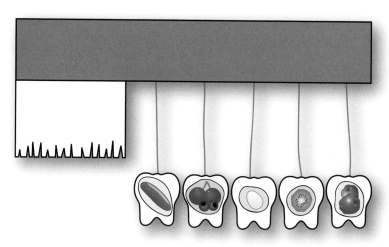

Steps:

1. Tape the index card to one end of the toothbrush handle; then snip the opposite edge of the card so it resembles toothbrush bristles.
2. Cut pictures of healthy foods from the magazine and glue each picture to a tooth.
3. Tape one end of a length of floss to the back of each tooth and the other end to the toothbrush handle.

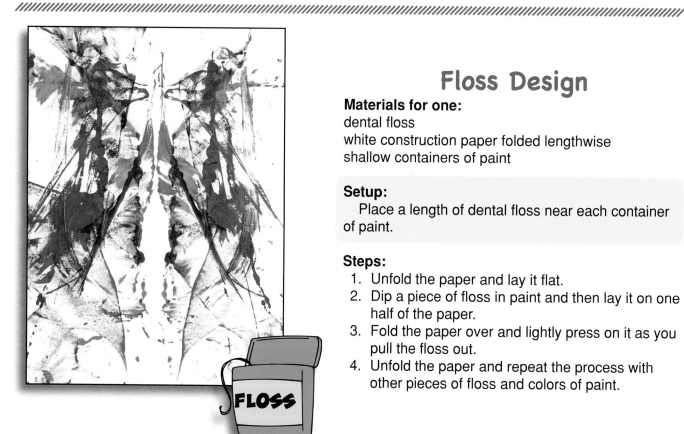

Floss Design

Materials for one:

dental floss
white construction paper folded lengthwise
shallow containers of paint

Setup:

　Place a length of dental floss near each container of paint.

Steps:

1. Unfold the paper and lay it flat.
2. Dip a piece of floss in paint and then lay it on one half of the paper.
3. Fold the paper over and lightly press on it as you pull the floss out.
4. Unfold the paper and repeat the process with other pieces of floss and colors of paint.

Winter

Toothy Smile

Materials for one:
cardboard egg carton
6" x 9" red construction paper   paintbrushes
white and pink paint   squeeze bottle
scissors   of glue

Setup:
   Cut a row of four egg cups from the egg carton. Trim the paper so it resembles lips, as shown.

Steps:
1. Paint the outside of the egg cups white so they resemble healthy teeth.
2. Paint the space between the cups pink (gums). Let the paint dry.
3. Squeeze glue along the straight edge of the carton; then press the lips on the glue so the teeth show through the opening.

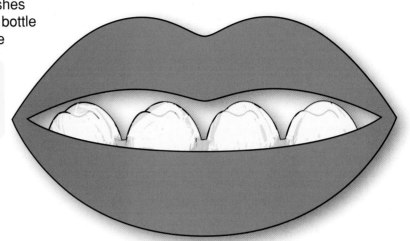

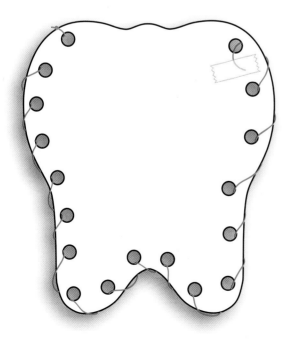

Remember to Floss

Materials for one:
thin, white polystyrene foam   hole puncher
   or tagboard tooth   tape
dental floss

Setup:
   Punch holes about one inch apart around the edge of the tooth. Tie a length of dental floss to one hole in the tooth.

Steps:
1. Lace the dental floss through each hole around the edge of the tooth.
2. When you are finished lacing, tape the loose end of the floss to the tooth.

Pearly White

Materials for one:
white corn syrup
toothbrush
tooth cut from 9" x 12" yellow construction paper
white paint

Setup:
Mix corn syrup in the paint.

Steps:
1. Dip the toothbrush in the paint mixture.
2. Brush the paint on the tooth, adding more paint to the brush as needed.

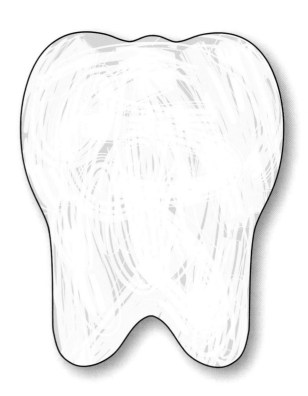

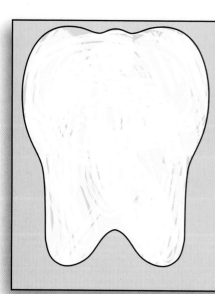

For Healthy Teeth, You Should...

Floss your teeth.
Brush your teeth.
Eat healthy food.
Go to the dentist.

Healthy Tooth Poster

Materials for one:
tooth painting (See the above idea.)
12" x 18" construction paper
glue
markers

Setup:
Program the paper with "For Healthy Teeth, You Should…"

Steps:
1. Glue the tooth on half of the paper.
2. On the opposite half of the paper, write or dictate things you should do to keep your teeth healthy.

"Hand-some" Lion

Materials for one:

construction paper lion face   paintbrushes
12" construction paper square   crayons
light brown and yellow paint   glue

Steps:

1. Paint one hand with the light brown paint. Make a circle of handprints on the paper, overlapping the palms.
2. Wash your hand; then repeat Step 1 with the yellow paint.
3. When the paint is dry, draw details on the lion face cutout and glue it to the center of the handprint mane.

Fluffy Lamb

Materials for one:

9" x 12" construction paper   black and white paint
green construction   paintbrushes
    paper scraps   glue
cotton balls   scissors

Steps:

1. Paint one hand black and make a handprint on the paper.
2. When the paint is dry, turn the paper upside down and glue cotton balls on and around the palm of the handprint.
3. Paint a small white eye on the thumb (head).
4. Cut green construction paper scraps into pieces (grass) and glue them below the handprint.

Shamrock Field

Materials for one:

3 corks
9" x 12" light green
   construction paper
rubber band

shallow container
   of green paint
green marker

Setup:

Wrap the rubber band around the corks as shown.

Steps:

1. Dip the corks in the paint and gently press them on the paper.
2. Repeat Step 1 until a desired number of prints are made.
3. When the paint is dry, use the green marker to add a stem to each print so it resembles a shamrock.

Colorful Rainbow

Materials for one:

black construction paper pot
white construction paper cloud
2 pieces of clear Con-Tact covering
tissue paper in rainbow colors
gold glitter

tape
glue
scissors

Setup:

Peel the backing from one piece of Con-Tact covering and tape it sticky side up to a work surface.

Steps:

1. Tear one color of tissue paper into small pieces and press the pieces on the Con-Tact covering to form an arc.
2. Repeat Step 1 with the remaining colors of tissue paper until the arcs look like a rainbow.
3. Spread glue along the top of the pot cutout. Sprinkle gold glitter on the glue and shake off the excess.
4. Press the pot on the Con-Tact covering at one end of the rainbow. Press the cloud at the other end.
5. Peel the backing off the other sheet of Con-Tact covering and smooth the sticky side over the project.
6. Trim the excess Con-Tact covering.

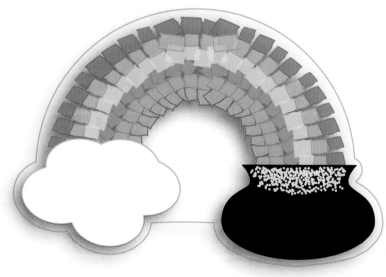

What a Treasure!

Materials for one:

lidded film canister   yellow paint
6" black pot cutout   glue
9" construction
     paper square
gold glitter

Steps:

1. Glue the pot cutout near the bottom of the square.
2. Dip one end of the film canister in the paint and gently press it above the pot to make a print that looks like a gold coin.
3. Repeat Step 2 until a desired number of coins are on the page.
4. While the paint is still wet, sprinkle gold glitter on the coins and then shake off the excess.

Lucky Clover

Materials for one:

four 3" green hearts   green glitter
5" construction paper circle   glue
green construction paper scrap   scissors

Steps:

1. Glue the hearts on the paper circle so they look like a four-leaf clover.
2. Cut a stem from the construction paper scrap and glue it in place.
3. Use the glue to make designs on the clover leaves.
4. Sprinkle glitter on the glue and shake off the excess.

Colorful Kite

Materials for one:

two 15" squares of clear
    Con-Tact covering
1" squares of colorful
    tissue paper

yarn
scissors
tape

Setup:

Remove the backing from one square of Con-Tact covering and tape it sticky-side up to a work surface.

Steps:

1. Place tissue paper squares on the Con-Tact covering until a desired effect is achieved.
2. Cut a length of yarn (tail) and place one end of it near the bottom center of the square.
3. Top the project with the other square of Con-Tact covering (backing removed), smoothing it with your hands to seal it.
4. Place the project so the yarn is at the bottom; then cut it into a kite shape.

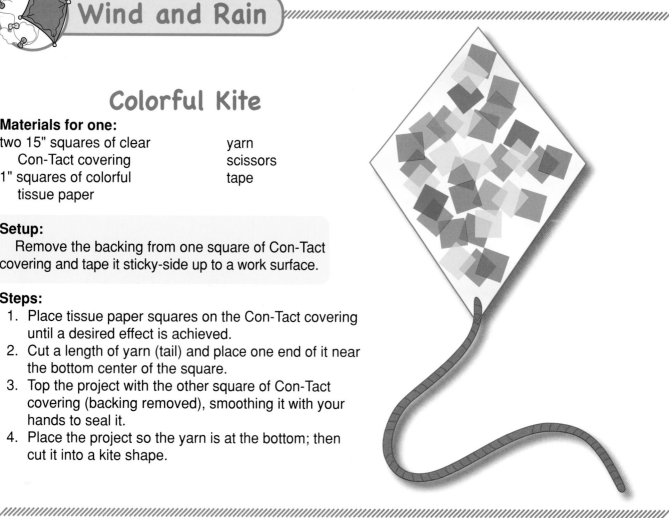

Blowing in the Wind

Materials for one:

sheet of newspaper
9" x 12" construction paper
construction paper scraps

scissors
crayons
glue

Steps:

1. Cut from the sheet of newspaper several small rectangles.
2. Cut from the paper scraps a few objects that could be blown by the wind, such as a hat, an umbrella, and a kite.
3. Draw a windy scene on the construction paper.
4. Glue the newspaper pieces and objects to the scene so they look as though they are being blown by the wind.

Stormy Painting

Materials for one:
18" length of waxed paper
white and black paint
2 plastic spoons

Steps:
1. Place a spoonful of each paint color in the center of the waxed paper.
2. Fingerpaint on the waxed paper, mixing the two colors as much as possible.
3. Use your fingers to make swirls in the paint.

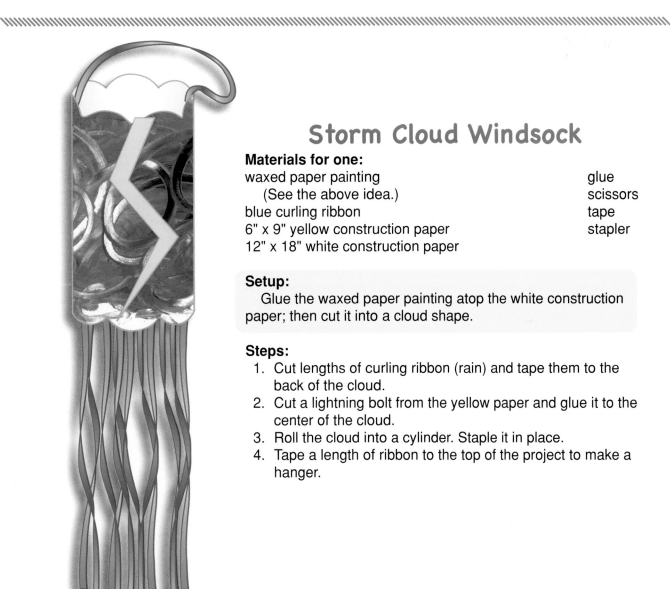

Storm Cloud Windsock

Materials for one:

waxed paper painting
   (See the above idea.)
blue curling ribbon
6" x 9" yellow construction paper
12" x 18" white construction paper

glue
scissors
tape
stapler

Setup:
   Glue the waxed paper painting atop the white construction paper; then cut it into a cloud shape.

Steps:
1. Cut lengths of curling ribbon (rain) and tape them to the back of the cloud.
2. Cut a lightning bolt from the yellow paper and glue it to the center of the cloud.
3. Roll the cloud into a cylinder. Staple it in place.
4. Tape a length of ribbon to the top of the project to make a hanger.

Raindrops Keep Falling

Materials for one:

12" x 18" gray
    construction paper
blue ink pad

black marker
crayons

Setup:

Use the marker to draw clouds at the top of the paper and label it as shown. Then draw a head and neck at the bottom of the page.

Steps:

1. Use crayons to draw hair and facial features on the head so they look like yours.
2. Press one fingertip on the blue ink pad and then on the paper (raindrop).
3. Repeat Step 2 to make a desired number of raindrops.

Under Cover

Materials for one:

paper cupcake liner
9" x 12" construction paper

glue
crayons

Steps:

1. Fold the cupcake liner in half and glue it near the center of the paper (set vertically), fluted side down.
2. Draw yourself below the cupcake liner as if you are holding an umbrella.
3. Draw a handle connecting the cupcake liner (umbrella) to your hand.
4. Draw a rainy scene on the remainder of the page.

Rain, Rain, Rain!

Materials for one:

seashell pasta tinted blue   scissors
light blue construction paper   glue
white tissue paper

Steps:

1. Cut a cloud from the tissue paper and glue it near the top of the paper.
2. Glue pieces of pasta (raindrops) below the cloud.

Muddy Boots

Materials for one:

yellow construction paper copy of   brown paint
   the boot patterns on page 135   scissors
2" x 9" yellow construction   glue
   paper strip   crayons
9" x 12" light blue
   construction paper

Steps:

1. Trim the edges of the yellow paper strip so it looks like the bottom of a raincoat and glue it to the top of the blue paper (set vertically).
2. Cut out the boots and glue them near the center of the paper as shown.
3. Draw legs to connect the boots to the bottom of the raincoat.
4. Squirt brown paint at the bottom of the blue paper and fingerpaint a mud puddle, making sure to make the boots muddy as well.

Egg Roll

Materials for one:
cardboard box
plastic eggs
sheet of construction paper cut to fit
    inside the box
paint

Steps:
1. Put the paper inside the box.
2. Pour several colors of paint on the paper.
3. Place one or more plastic eggs in the box.
4. Gently tilt the box back and forth to roll the eggs through the paint.

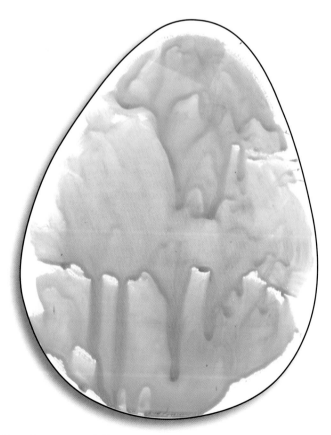

Shiny Easter Egg

Materials for one:

shallow containers of sweetened condensed milk	white tagboard egg cutout
food coloring	paintbrushes

Setup:
    To make sweet milk paint, use the food coloring to tint each container of sweetened condensed milk a different color.

Steps:
1. Paint the egg with different colors of sweet milk paint.
2. While the milk is still wet, tilt the egg so the colors blend.

A Chocolate Egg

Materials for one:
brown construction paper egg cutout
brown crayon
squeeze bottles of tinted glue

Steps:
1. Use the crayon to draw designs on the egg cutout.
2. Squeeze the glue over the designs.

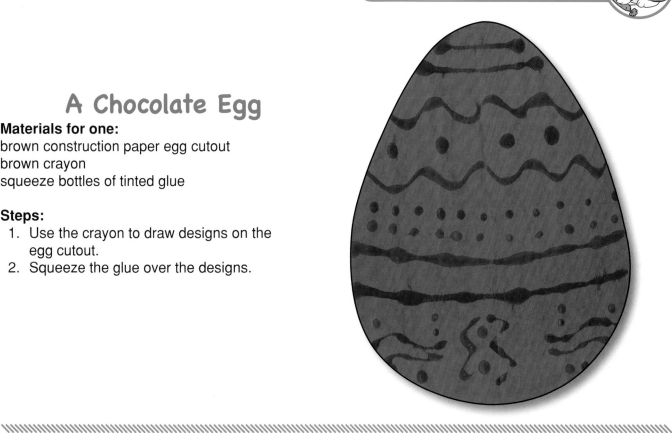

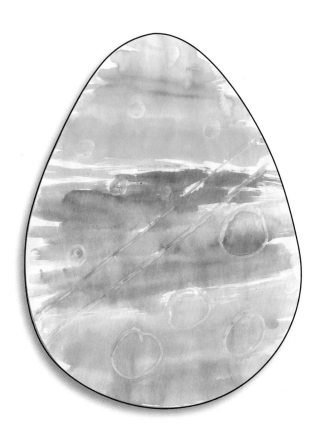

Stripes, Dots, and Spots

Materials for one:

white construction paper egg cutout
squeeze bottle of glue
watercolors
paintbrush

Steps:
1. Squeeze the glue to make designs on the egg.
2. When the glue is completely dry, paint over it with the watercolors to reveal the designs.

Hopping Away

Materials for one:

clean Styrofoam egg cartons
   cut into pieces
paper shreds or plastic
   Easter grass
basket cutout
4" white paper circle

9" x 12" construction paper
white construction
   paper scraps
cotton ball
glue
scissors

Steps:

1. Glue the basket cutout on one half of the paper.
2. Glue the paper shreds or Easter grass and Styrofoam egg carton pieces around the basket.
3. Glue the white circle (bunny) on the other half of the paper.
4. Glue the cotton ball on the center of the circle so it looks like a tail.
5. Cut ears from the paper scraps and glue them at the top of the circle as shown.

Fluffy Bunny

Materials for one:

nonmentholated shaving cream
9" x 12" construction paper
construction paper scraps

glue
scissors
marker

Setup:

To make puff paint, mix equal parts of shaving cream and glue.

Steps:

1. Use the puff paint to fingerpaint a bunny on the construction paper.
2. Cut facial features and other details from the construction paper scraps.
3. When the puff paint is dry, glue the details on the bunny. Use the marker to embellish the details as desired.

Bunny Box

Materials for one:

clean individual-size milk
   carton with the top cut off
construction paper scraps

cotton balls
scissors
glue

Steps:

1. Glue cotton balls to the outside of the milk carton until the sides are completely covered.
2. When the glue is dry, cut facial features and body parts from the construction paper scraps and glue them to the milk carton so it looks like a bunny.

Hop, Hop, Hop

Materials for one:

copy of the bunny body parts
   patterns from page 135
toilet tissue tube
white pom-pom
white paint

paintbrush
crayons
scissors
glue

Steps:

1. Paint the cardboard tube white.
2. When the paint is dry, color and cut out the patterns and glue them to the tube as shown.
3. Glue the pom-pom to the back of the tube.

Spring and Summer

Lots of Flies

Materials for one:
copy of the frog pattern
   on page 136
9" x 12" light blue
   construction paper
white construction
   paper scraps
medium-size black
   pom-poms
crayons
scissors
glue

Steps:
1. Color and cut out the frog. Glue it to the sheet of construction paper.
2. From the paper scraps, cut out pairs of wings.
3. To make each fly, glue a pair of wings and a pom-pom to the paper as shown.

Funny Frog

Materials for one:
large green construction paper circle (body)
large green construction paper oval (head)
2 small white paper circles
four 1" x 12" green construction paper strips
black marker
glue

Steps:
1. To make eyes, color a black circle on each white circle. Glue the eyes to the head as shown.
2. Draw a mouth on the head and then glue the head to the body.
3. Accordion-fold the paper strips and glue them to the body so they look like legs.

A Little Pond

Materials for one:

blue and green tissue
  paper scraps
paper plate

pond-related craft
  foam shapes
diluted glue
paintbrush

Steps:

1. Brush the center of the paper plate with diluted glue.
2. Cover the glue with small pieces of blue tissue paper.
3. Brush glue along the edge of the plate.
4. Cover the glue with small pieces of green tissue paper.
5. Glue desired craft foam shapes to the pond.

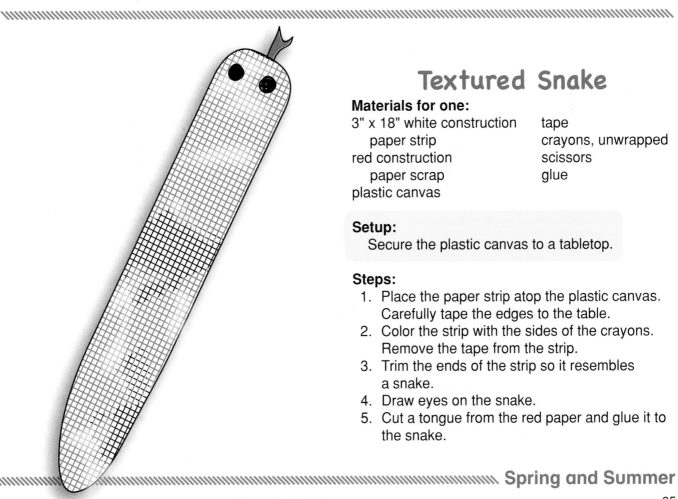

Textured Snake

Materials for one:

3" x 18" white construction
  paper strip
red construction
  paper scrap
plastic canvas

tape
crayons, unwrapped
scissors
glue

Setup:

  Secure the plastic canvas to a tabletop.

Steps:

1. Place the paper strip atop the plastic canvas. Carefully tape the edges to the table.
2. Color the strip with the sides of the crayons. Remove the tape from the strip.
3. Trim the ends of the strip so it resembles a snake.
4. Draw eyes on the snake.
5. Cut a tongue from the red paper and glue it to the snake.

Spring and Summer

Swimming Along

Materials for one:

9" x 12" white construction paper
blue and orange paint
paintbrush
scissors
fine-tip black marker

Steps:

1. Paint the white paper blue. Allow the paint to dry.
2. Cut one edge of the paper to look like waves.
3. Dip your thumb in the orange paint and press it on the paper to make a print (body). Then dip your finger in the paint and make a print (tail) beside the thumbprint.
4. Repeat Step 3 to make several more fish on the paper. Allow the paint to dry.
5. Use the marker to add details to the fish.

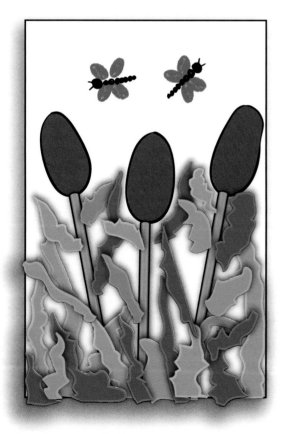

Dragonflies and Cattails

Materials for one:

nonmentholated shaving cream
3 green straws
12" x 18" white construction paper
brown and green construction paper scraps
plastic spoon
brown and purple paint
glue
black marker

Setup:

Mix equal parts of brown paint and white glue. Then add shaving cream.

Steps:

1. Spoon three blobs of the shaving cream mixture on the paper. Shape the blobs so they resemble cattails. Allow the mixture to dry.
2. Glue a straw below each cattail.
3. Tear the paper scraps to make leaves and tall grass and then glue them around the cattails.
4. Above the cattails, draw two sets of connecting circles (dragonfly bodies). Draw antennae on each body.
5. Dip your thumb in purple paint and make prints beside the bodies so they resemble wings.

Mom and Her Babies

Materials for one:

black and orange construction
paper scraps
paper plate
large yellow pom-pom
5 medium-size yellow
pom-poms
large craft stick
5 regular-size craft sticks
blue paint
paintbrush
scissors
glue

Setup:

Cut a long slit in the center of the plate. About 1½ inches in front of the long slit, cut five short slits.

Steps:

1. Paint the front of the paper plate blue. Allow the paint to dry.
2. Cut from the paper scraps a pair of eyes and a beak for each pom-pom (duck). Glue the eyes and beaks to the ducks.
3. Glue the large duck to the large craft stick and the smaller ducks to regular-size craft sticks.
4. Insert the large duck's craft stick in the long slit. Insert each of the remaining ducks' craft sticks in a small slit. *(If desired, lead students in singing "Five Little Ducks," encouraging youngsters to remove a baby duck after each verse.)*

A Cattail Masterpiece

Materials for one:

real or artificial cattails
12" x 18" white construction paper
containers of blue, green, and brown paint

Steps:

1. Roll a cattail in one color of paint to cover it completely.
2. Roll, press, or drag the cattail on the paper.
3. Repeat Steps 1 and 2 with different colors.

Spring and Summer

Smiling Flower

Materials for one:

3" construction paper triangles
   in various colors
paper plate
large craft stick

scissors
glue
green marker
tape

Setup:
  Cut the center from the paper plate.

Steps:

1. Glue triangles around the edge of the plate so they resemble flower petals.
2. Color the craft stick. Tape the stick to the back of the paper plate.
3. Hold the flower and look through the center. Smile!

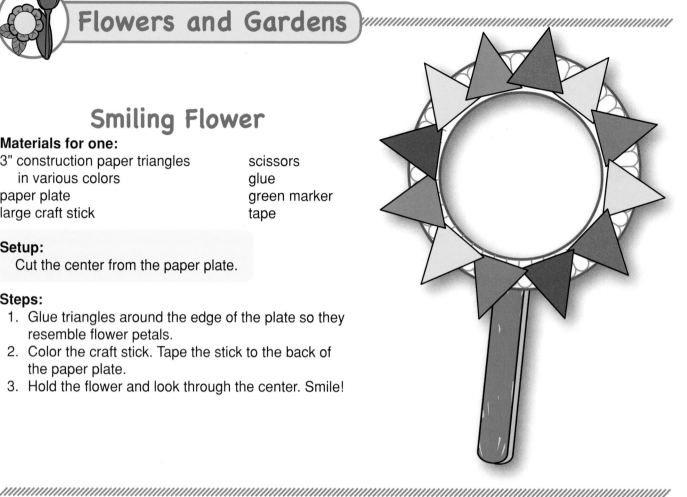

Floral Prints

Materials for one:

white construction paper
green marker
shallow containers of different-colored paint
wipes

Steps:

1. On the paper, draw several stems with leaves.
2. Dip your finger in the paint and make prints so they resemble a flower at the top of each stem. Use the wipes to clean your fingers between making prints of different colors.

Splattered Flower

Materials for one:

1½" x 9" green construction
    paper strip (stem)
green construction paper
    scraps
spray bottles
paper plate
coffee filter
different colors of
    diluted paint
glue
scissors

Setup:

Pour a different color of paint into each spray bottle.

Steps:

1. Spray the plate and the coffee filter with each color of paint until a desired effect is achieved. Allow the paint to dry.
2. Crumple the coffee filter and glue its center to the middle of the plate.
3. Glue the stem to the back of the plate.
4. Cut leaves from the paper scraps and then glue them to the stem.

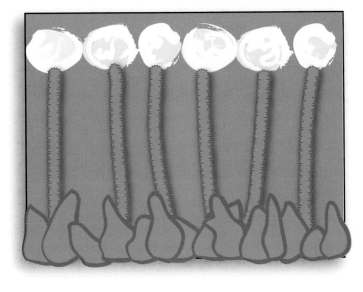

Dandelions in a Row

Materials for one:

9" x 12" blue
    construction paper
green construction
    paper scraps
6 lengths of green
    pipe cleaner
large pom-pom
glue
white paint

Steps:

1. On the blue paper, glue the pipe cleaners in a line, leaving space between them.
2. Dip the pom-pom in the paint and make a print at the top of each pipe cleaner.
3. Tear paper scraps and glue them to the bottom of the paper so they resemble grass.

Spring and Summer

Vegetable Patch

Materials for one:

9" x 12" brown
   construction paper
colorful tissue
   paper squares

craft stick
brown paint
glue

Steps:

1. Dip the craft stick in the paint and brush it across the brown paper to make lines that resemble the rows of a garden.
2. For each row, crumple same-colored tissue paper squares and glue them to the paper so they look like vegetables growing.

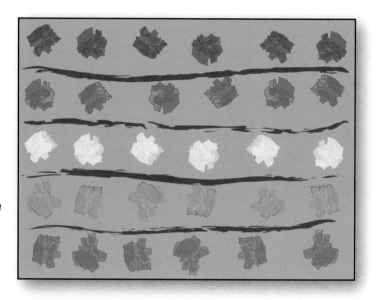

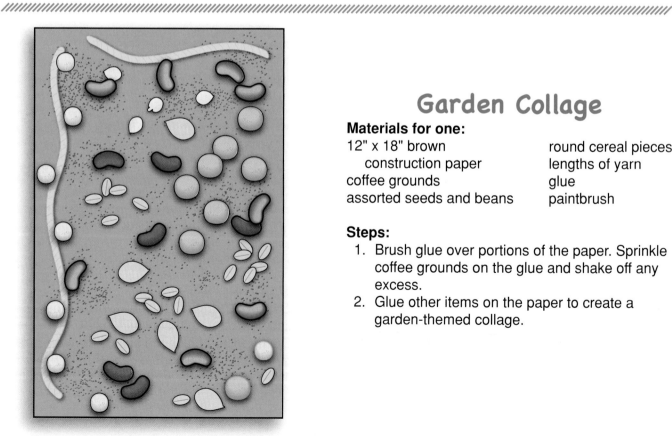

Garden Collage

Materials for one:

12" x 18" brown
   construction paper
coffee grounds
assorted seeds and beans

round cereal pieces
lengths of yarn
glue
paintbrush

Steps:

1. Brush glue over portions of the paper. Sprinkle coffee grounds on the glue and shake off any excess.
2. Glue other items on the paper to create a garden-themed collage.

Recycled Sculpture

Materials for one:

cardboard square   food coloring
recycled paper, shredded   glue

Setup:

Mix a few drops of food coloring into each of several bottles of glue.

Steps:

1. Arrange shredded paper on the cardboard square.
2. Squirt one or more colors of glue on the paper.
3. Add more paper and glue, as desired, to create layers in the sculpture.

Under the Sun

Materials for one:

used magazines   green crayon
12" x 18" construction paper   scissors
shallow container of yellow paint   glue

Steps:

1. Place your hand in the paint and then make a circle of prints on the paper to form a sun. Allow the paint to dry.
2. Color the portion of the paper below the sun (grass).
3. Cut pictures of plants and animals from the magazines.
4. Glue the pictures to the paper.

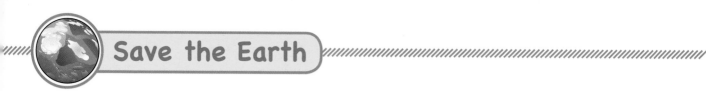

Helping Hands

Materials for one:

9" x 12" flesh-tone construction paper
paper plate
coffee filter
spray bottle of water
green and blue washable markers
scissors
glue

Steps:

1. Use the markers to color the coffee filter. Spray the filter with water and then allow it to dry.
2. Glue the filter to the bottom of the paper plate.
3. On the paper, trace your hands and cut out the tracings.
4. Glue the hand cutouts to the filter as shown.

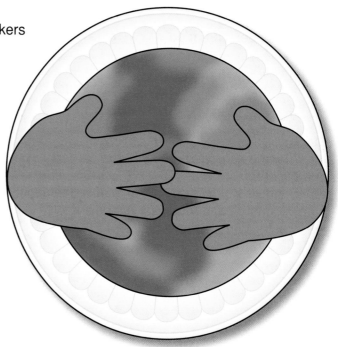

Modern Art

Materials for one:

shoebox lid
crayon sharpener
squeeze bottle of glue
used crayons

Steps:

1. Squeeze glue inside the lid to create a design.
2. Sharpen the crayons over the box, letting the shavings fall in the glue until the glue is covered.
3. If desired, add more glue and shavings.

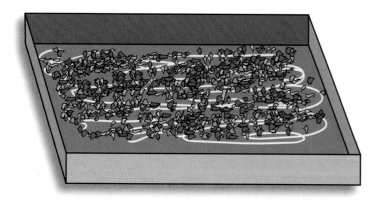

Marshmallow Caterpillars

Materials for one:
large marshmallows
9" x 12" construction paper
containers of paint
black marker

Steps:
1. Dip a marshmallow in paint and then press it on the paper to make a print.
2. Make several more connecting prints to form a caterpillar. Repeat with different marshmallows and colors of paint to form several caterpillars. Allow the paint to dry.
3. Use the marker to add details to the caterpillars.

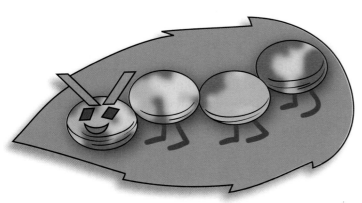

On a Leaf

Materials for one:
2 medicine droppers   glue
4 cotton cosmetic rounds   scissors
large green construction paper leaf   markers
construction paper scraps
paper plate
different colors of tinted water

Steps:
1. Place the cotton rounds on the paper plate and then drip the tinted water on the rounds. Allow the rounds to dry.
2. Glue the cotton rounds to the leaf so they resemble a caterpillar.
3. Use the paper scraps and markers to add facial details and legs to the caterpillar.

Colorful Caterpillar

Materials for one:

sterilized egg carton section
   (caterpillar)
construction paper scraps
two 2" lengths of black
   pipe cleaner

paint
sponges
glue
markers

Steps:

1. Sponge-paint the caterpillar. Allow the paint to dry.
2. Push the pipe cleaners through one end of the caterpillar so they resemble antennae.
3. Use the paper scraps and markers to add other details.

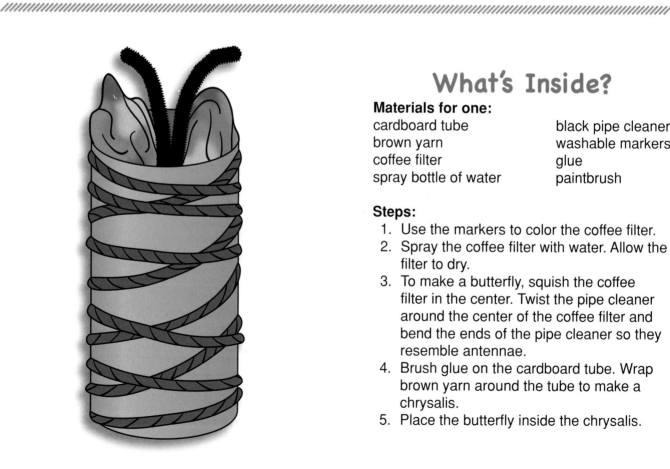

What's Inside?

Materials for one:

cardboard tube
brown yarn
coffee filter
spray bottle of water

black pipe cleaner
washable markers
glue
paintbrush

Steps:

1. Use the markers to color the coffee filter.
2. Spray the coffee filter with water. Allow the filter to dry.
3. To make a butterfly, squish the coffee filter in the center. Twist the pipe cleaner around the center of the coffee filter and bend the ends of the pipe cleaner so they resemble antennae.
4. Brush glue on the cardboard tube. Wrap brown yarn around the tube to make a chrysalis.
5. Place the butterfly inside the chrysalis.

Butterfly Bag

Materials for one:

sheet of newspaper
2" x 9" construction paper
   strip (handle)
paper lunch bag
pipe cleaner

paint
paintbrushes
tape
stapler

Steps:

1. Paint the newspaper and the paper bag. Allow the paint to dry.
2. To make a butterfly, accordion-fold the newspaper and then twist the pipe cleaner around its center. Bend the ends of the pipe cleaner so they look like antennae.
3. Tape the butterfly to the bag.
4. Staple the handle to the bag.

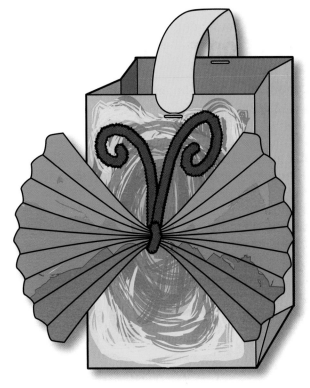

Spotted Butterfly

Materials for one:

tagboard butterfly tracer
9" x 12" white construction paper
construction paper scraps
paint

paintbrushes
glue
hole puncher
scissors

Setup:
   Mix a small amount of glue in each color of paint.

Steps:

1. Place the butterfly tracer on your paper and trace around the butterfly.
2. Hole-punch the paper scraps, saving the dots.
3. Paint the inside of the tracing. Sprinkle the dots on the wet paint. Allow the paint to dry.
4. Cut out the butterfly.

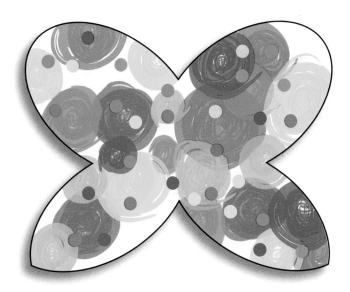

Spring and Summer

Designer Wings

Materials for one:
large construction paper butterfly
lengths of yarn
containers of colorful paint

Steps:
1. Dip a length of yarn in paint, coating all but the tip of the yarn.
2. Arrange the yarn on one wing as desired. Fold the butterfly so one wing is atop the other wing and press the wings together.
3. Leaving the butterfly folded, gently pull the yarn from between the wings.
4. Unfold the butterfly.
5. Repeat Steps 1–4 using a different color of paint.

Butterfly Wreath

Materials for one:

2" black construction paper square	glue
brightly colored tissue paper rectangles	paintbrush
green tissue paper scraps	scissors
paper plate, center removed	

Steps:
1. Brush glue over the inside of the paper plate.
2. Tear the tissue paper scraps and place the pieces on the glue.
3. Twist a few rectangles to look like butterflies and glue them on the plate.
4. Cut the square into thin strips. Then fold each strip so it resembles antennae and glue a strip to each butterfly.

Ladybugs on a Leaf

Materials for one:
3 sterilized egg carton sections
large green construction paper leaf
construction paper eyes
cotton swab
six 1" lengths of pipe cleaner
red and black paint
paintbrush
glue

Steps:
1. To make ladybugs, paint the egg carton sections red.
2. Dip the cotton swab in black paint and make dots on the ladybugs. Allow the paint to dry.
3. Glue the eyes to the ladybugs. Then push the pipe cleaners in at the top of the ladybugs so they look like antennae.
4. Glue the ladybugs on the leaf.

Beautiful Beetle

Materials for one:

construction paper scraps	scissors
paper bowl	glue
paint	markers
paintbrushes	

Steps:
1. Paint the bottom and sides of the bowl as desired. Allow the paint to dry.
2. Cut eyes, legs, and antennae from the paper scraps and glue them on the bowl.
3. Use the paper scraps and markers to add stripes or spots to the bowl.

Spring and Summer

Buzzing Bee

Materials for one:

3 small paper plates   paintbrushes
2 coffee filters (wings)   stapler
2 black pipe cleaner halves markers
yellow and black paint   hole puncher

Steps:

1. Paint the back of each paper plate yellow. Paint black stripes on two of the plates. Allow the paint to dry.
2. To make a bee, staple the plates together as shown. Then staple the wings to the center plate.
3. Draw a face on the top plate.
4. Punch two holes near the top of the bee and one hole near the bottom. Thread a pipe cleaner through the holes at the top and twist it so its ends look like antennae. Thread a pipe cleaner through the hole near the bottom and twist it so it resembles a stinger.

Baby Birds

Materials for one:

brown paper shreds   brown crayon
construction paper scraps   glue
paper bowl   paintbrush
3 large pom-poms   scissors

Steps:

1. Use the brown crayon to color the outside of the bowl.
2. Brush glue on the inside of the bowl. Then fill the bowl with the paper shreds.
3. To make birds, cut eyes and beaks from the paper scraps and then glue two eyes and a beak to each pom-pom.
4. Glue the birds on the paper shreds.

Little Blue Bird

Materials for one:
2" blue construction paper circle
9" x 12" blue construction paper
blue and orange construction paper scraps
small paper plate half
crayons
scissors
glue

Steps:
1. Use a blue crayon to color the paper plate.
2. On the sheet of blue construction paper, trace your hands. Cut out the tracings.
3. Glue the cutouts and the paper circle to the paper plate so they resemble wings and a head.
4. Draw an eye on the head. Then cut a beak and a tail from the paper scraps and glue them to the bird.

Feathery Friend

Materials for one:

construction paper scraps	glue
2 craft sticks	scissors
craft feathers	markers
two 2" lengths of orange pipe cleaner	

Steps:
1. Glue the crafts sticks together to form a lowercase *t*. Allow the glue to dry.
2. Cover the craft sticks by gluing feathers on them.
3. Use the paper scraps and markers to make a bird face. Glue the face to the craft sticks.
4. Bend the pipe cleaners so they resemble legs and feet. Then glue them near the bottom of the vertical craft stick.

Spring and Summer

A Frame for Mom

Materials for one:

CD case
2 construction paper squares
    sized to fit in the case
construction paper scraps

photo of the child
glue
markers
crayons

Steps:

1. Glue the photo in the center of one paper square.
2. Write a message on the other paper square.
3. Use the paper scraps, markers, and crayons to further decorate the squares.
4. Slip a paper square into each side of the CD case.

Special Bouquet

Materials for one:

3 gift bows
green paper scraps
paper cup
3 craft sticks

scissors
markers
crayons
glue

Setup:

In the bottom of the cup, cut three slits large enough for a craft stick to fit through.

Steps:

1. Turn the paper cup upside down and use the markers and crayons to decorate it.
2. Use a green marker to color the craft sticks.
3. To make each flower, glue a gift bow to a craft stick. Cut leaves from the paper scraps and glue them to the craft stick stem.
4. Insert each flower in a slit.

Pencil Holder

Materials for one:
clean empty can with no sharp edges
white paper strip sized to fit around the can
small photo of the child
containers of paint
shaped sponges
crayons
permanent black marker
glue

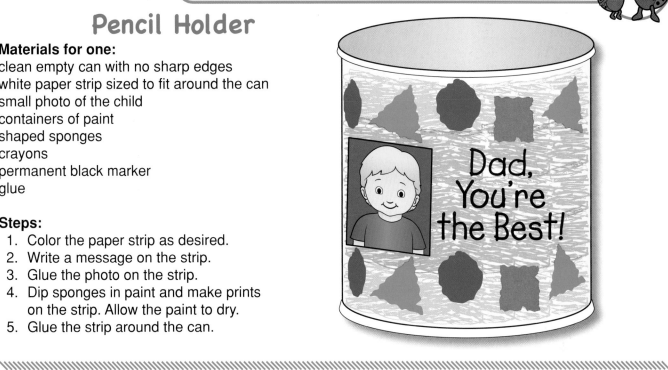

Steps:
1. Color the paper strip as desired.
2. Write a message on the strip.
3. Glue the photo on the strip.
4. Dip sponges in paint and make prints on the strip. Allow the paint to dry.
5. Glue the strip around the can.

A Sharp-Dressed Card

Materials for one:

9" x 12" construction paper	small photo of the child
4½" x 12" fingerpaint paper strip	2 large buttons
	scissors
2 construction paper triangles	fingerpaint
	glue
	permanent black marker

Setup:
Lay a button on the photo and trace around it. Then cut out the tracing.

Steps:
1. Paint the paper strip. Allow the paint to dry. Cut a necktie shape from the strip (with help as needed).
2. Write "Who Loves You?" on the tie.
3. Glue the buttons and the photo in a line down the center of the construction paper.
4. Write "Me!" under the photo.
5. Glue the triangles and tie to the paper as shown.

Spring and Summer

Oops!

Materials for one:
copy of a poem card from page 136
plastic canvas
fingerpaint paper
light brown construction paper square
construction paper scraps
brown fingerpaint
scissors
unwrapped brown crayon
hole puncher
glue

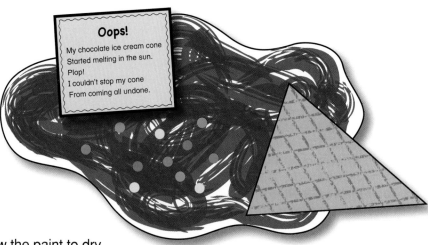

Oops!
My chocolate ice cream cone
Started melting in the sun.
Plop!
I couldn't stop my cone
From coming all undone.

Steps:
1. Paint on the fingerpaint paper. Allow the paint to dry.
2. Cut around the edge of the painted paper so it looks like melted ice cream.
3. Place the paper square atop the canvas. Then rub the side of the crayon over it. Cut an ice cream cone shape from the paper (with help as needed).
4. To make sprinkles, hole-punch the paper scraps.
5. Glue the sprinkles, cone, and poem to the melted ice cream.

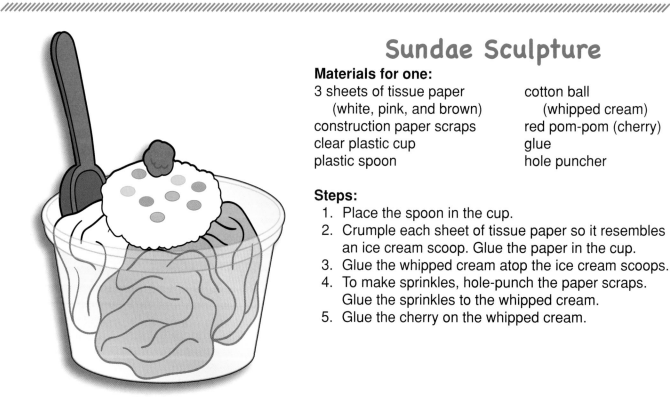

Sundae Sculpture

Materials for one:
3 sheets of tissue paper
  (white, pink, and brown)
construction paper scraps
clear plastic cup
plastic spoon

cotton ball
  (whipped cream)
red pom-pom (cherry)
glue
hole puncher

Steps:
1. Place the spoon in the cup.
2. Crumple each sheet of tissue paper so it resembles an ice cream scoop. Glue the paper in the cup.
3. Glue the whipped cream atop the ice cream scoops.
4. To make sprinkles, hole-punch the paper scraps. Glue the sprinkles to the whipped cream.
5. Glue the cherry on the whipped cream.

Spring and Summer

A Big Scoop

Materials for one:
nonmentholated shaving cream
food coloring
white construction paper bowl cutout
8" construction paper square
resealable plastic bag
crayons
glue
scissors

Setup:
Place equal parts of shaving cream and glue in the resealable plastic bag. Add a few drops of food coloring and then seal the bag.

Steps:
1. Color the bowl and then glue it to the paper square.
2. Squish the plastic bag to mix its contents. Cut a small hole in the corner of the bag (with help as needed).
3. Squeeze the mixture onto the paper so it looks like ice cream in the bowl.

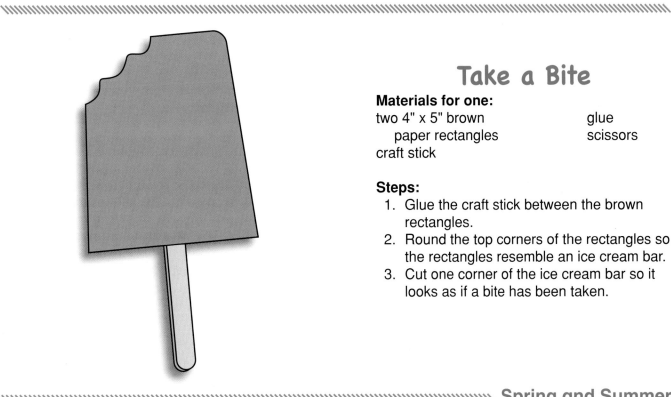

Take a Bite

Materials for one:

two 4" x 5" brown paper rectangles	glue scissors
craft stick	

Steps:
1. Glue the craft stick between the brown rectangles.
2. Round the top corners of the rectangles so the rectangles resemble an ice cream bar.
3. Cut one corner of the ice cream bar so it looks as if a bite has been taken.

Spring and Summer

Flip-Flop Prints

Materials for one:

pair of child-size flip-flops   damp sponge
craft sand   shallow container of
seashells   light brown paint
tan construction paper   shallow container of glue
craft feather

Steps:

1. Dip the bottom of a flip-flop in the paint and press it on the paper.
2. Repeat with the remaining flip-flop; then sprinkle sand on the wet prints.
3. Repeat Steps 1 and 2 to make another set of prints.
4. Dip the sponge in the glue and press it on the paper around the prints; then sprinkle sand on the glue.
5. Glue the shells and feather to the paper.

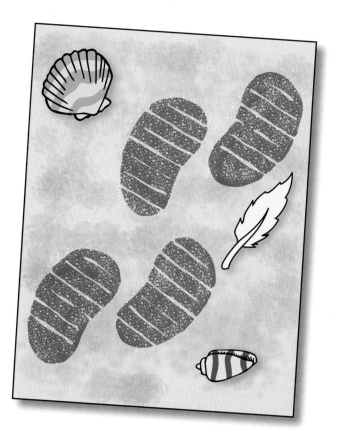

Shimmering Fish

Materials for one:

2 squares of clear Con-Tact covering
aluminum foil triangle (fin)
1" colorful tissue paper squares
glitter
scissors
permanent marker

Steps:

1. Peel the backing off a Con-Tact covering square and place it sticky-side up on a table.
2. Press the tissue paper and the fin on the square; then sprinkle on a very small amount of glitter.
3. Peel the backing off the remaining square and press it on the decorated square. Cut a simple fish shape from the square (with help as needed).
4. Draw eye and mouth details.

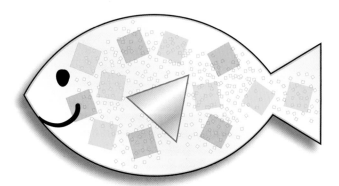

Resting Seagull

Materials for one:
3" x 4" brown rectangle (post)
9" x 12" blue construction paper
white and yellow construction paper scraps
small paper plate half (body)
gray craft feathers
thin twine or light brown yarn
scissors
black crayon
glue

Steps:
1. Glue the post to the bottom of the blue paper.
2. Glue the curved edge of the body to the top of the post.
3. Cut a head from the white paper scraps and glue it to the body; then cut a beak from the yellow scraps and glue it to the head. Draw eye details.
4. Glue gray feathers to the middle and back of the body.
5. Cut pieces of twine and glue them to the post so they resemble rope.

Cool Beach Towel

Materials for one:
construction paper person
9" x 12" white construction paper folded in half
squeeze bottles of paint
crayons
glue

Steps:
1. Unfold the paper; then squeeze thin lines of paint on one side of the fold.
2. Refold the paper and gently rub your hand across it. Unfold it and let the paint dry.
3. Draw a bathing suit, hair, and facial details on the person.
4. Glue the person to the paper.

Crafty Sand Castle

Materials for one:

sturdy box lid
craft sand
seashells
small paper rectangle
small disposable cup with a
    hole poked in the bottom

small paper bowl
6" pipe cleaner
wide paintbrush
glue

Setup:

Pour sand in the box lid. To make the castle, glue the cup upside down to the bottom of the bowl.

Steps:

1. Brush glue on the castle.
2. Hold the castle over the box and pour sand on the wet glue.
3. Glue seashells to the castle.
4. Glue the rectangle to one end of the pipe cleaner to make a flag; then slide the flag in the cup hole.

Seashell Rubbings

Materials for one:

seashell clip art
tagboard
white copy paper

squeeze bottle of glue
unwrapped crayons
tape

Setup:

Copy the shells onto tagboard. Use the glue to trace the shell details. Let the glue dry. Tape the tagboard to a table.

Steps:

1. Tape the paper over the tagboard.
2. Rub the side of a crayon over the paper.
3. Use crayons to add details to the rubbing.

Seaside Sunset

Materials for one:
small yellow semicircle (sun)
4½" x 12" white construction paper
9" x 12" blue construction paper
red, orange, and yellow paint
small foam paint roller
glue
blue marker

Steps:

1. Glue the white paper to the top half of the blue paper.
2. Put a dollop of each paint color on one side of the white paper.
3. To make the sunset, use the roller to spread the paint across the white paper. Let the paint dry.
4. Glue the sun to the bottom edge of the sunset.
5. Draw waves on the blue paper.

Beach Bottle

Materials for one:
clear plastic bottle with cap (wrapper removed)
plastic funnel
small scooper
sand
assorted craft materials, such as small shells,
    aquarium gravel or pebbles, and small feathers
gold glitter
craft glue

Steps:

1. Place the funnel in the bottle opening.
2. Use the scooper to pour sand in the funnel, filling the bottle about halfway.
3. Add craft items and glitter to the bottle.
4. Spread a small amount of glue on the inside of the cap; then screw the cap on the bottle.
4. Tilt the bottle to move the craft items around in the sand.

Spring and Summer

Amazing Sea Critter

Materials for one:

construction paper
sea animal templates
yarn

squeeze bottle of glue
scissors
crayons

Steps:

1. Draw or trace a sea critter outline on the paper.
2. Squeeze glue on the outline; then cut yarn and place it on the glue. Let the glue dry.
3. Use crayons to add details to the project.

Jolly Jellyfish

Materials for one:

2 semicircles of clear Con-Tact covering
1" colorful tissue paper squares
waxed paper
scissors

Steps:

1. Peel the backing off a semicircle and place it sticky-side up on a table.
2. Press tissue paper squares on the semicircle.
3. Cut waxed paper strips and press them on the straight edge of the semicircle so they resemble tentacles.
4. Peel the backing off the remaining semicircle and press it on the decorated semicircle.
5. Trim any excess tissue paper from the curved edge.

Hot Dog With the Works

Materials for one:
red construction paper hot dog
tan construction paper bun
9" x 12" sheet of paper
green paper confetti (pickles)
white paper shreds (sauerkraut)
squeeze bottle of red paint (ketchup)
squeeze bottle of yellow paint (mustard)
glue

Steps:
1. Glue the hot dog and bun to the sheet of paper.
2. Glue pickles to the hot dog.
3. Glue sauerkraut to the hot dog.
4. Squirt ketchup and mustard over the hot dog.

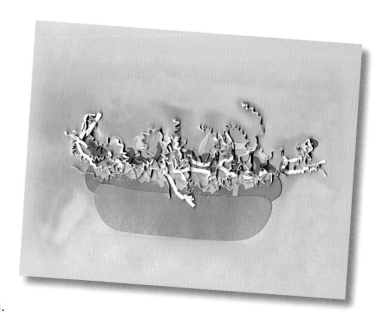

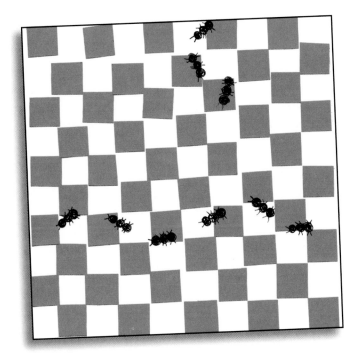

Unexpected Guests

Materials for one:
10" white construction paper square
fifty 1" red construction paper squares
black marker
glue

Steps:
1. Glue the red squares to the white square to make a checkerboard pattern.
2. Use the marker to draw ants.

S'more Sculpture

Materials for one:
powdered cocoa mix
two 3" cardboard squares
two 2" brown craft foam squares
napkin
3 cotton balls
glue

Steps:
1. Glue a foam square to a cardboard square.
2. Glue the cotton balls to the foam square.
3. Sprinkle cocoa on the cotton balls.
4. Glue the remaining foam square on top of the cotton balls.
5. Glue the remaining cardboard square to the foam square.
6. Glue the resulting s'more to the napkin.

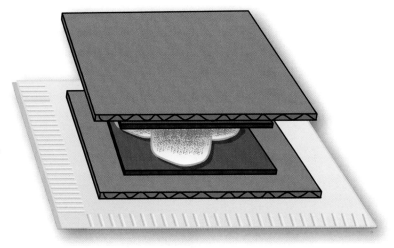

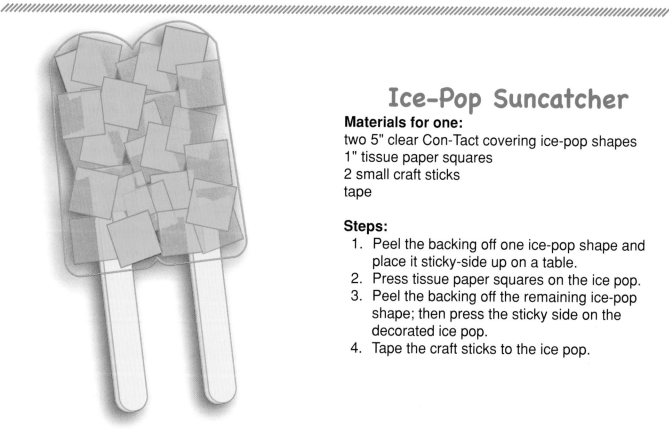

Ice-Pop Suncatcher

Materials for one:
two 5" clear Con-Tact covering ice-pop shapes
1" tissue paper squares
2 small craft sticks
tape

Steps:
1. Peel the backing off one ice-pop shape and place it sticky-side up on a table.
2. Press tissue paper squares on the ice pop.
3. Peel the backing off the remaining ice-pop shape; then press the sticky side on the decorated ice pop.
4. Tape the craft sticks to the ice pop.

Spring and Summer

Serving Cheeseburgers

Materials for one:
spatula
2" orange or yellow construction paper squares (cheese)
9" x 12" construction paper
3" round sponge
shallow containers of green and brown paint
glue

Setup:
Place the spatula next to the green paint. Place the sponge next to the brown paint.

Steps:
1. Dip the spatula in the green paint and then press it on the paper. Repeat several times.
2. Dip the sponge in the brown paint and then press it on a spatula print. Repeat the process for each spatula print.
3. Glue cheese on each sponge print.

The Ants Go Marching

Materials for one:
brown and white uncooked rice
kitchen sponge
6" x 18" green construction paper strip
black hole-punched dots (eyes)
shallow container of red paint
red and green crayons
glue
scissors

Setup:
Cut the sponge to make an ant-shaped printer.

Steps:
1. Dip the sponge in the paint and then press it on the paper several times to make ants, adding more paint to the sponge as needed.
2. For each ant, press two eyes on the wet paint.
3. Use the red crayon to draw legs and antennae.
4. Use the green crayon to draw grass around the ants.
5. Glue rice (food crumbs) on the paper.

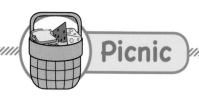

Picnic

Ice-Cold Lemonade

Materials for one:

kitchen sponge
clear plastic deli container lid
plastic film canister
6" x 9" construction paper
shallow containers of yellow
   and red paint

glue
red marker
scissors

Setup:
   Cut the sponge to make a tumbler-shaped printer. Cut the plastic lid into one-inch squares (ice cubes).

Steps:
1. Dip the sponge in the yellow paint and press it on the paper.
2. Glue ice cubes to the print.
3. Dip the film canister in the red paint and press it near the top of the print to make a cherry.
4. Draw a stem on the cherry.

Picnic Surprise

Materials for one:

copy of the picnic basket
   patterns on page 138
plastic canvas
grocery store circular
9" x 12" construction paper

unwrapped brown crayon
scissors
glue
marker
tape

Setup:
   Tape the canvas to a tabletop. Tape the pattern page over the canvas.

Steps:
1. Rub the side of the crayon over the patterns.
2. Cut out the patterns. Glue the bottom of the picnic basket to the paper. Set the lid to the side.
3. Cut pictures of picnic foods from the circular and glue them to the paper above the basket.
4. Glue the top edge of the lid to the paper, leaving the bottom unattached to make a flap.
5. Write "What's inside" on the picnic basket lid and "my picnic basket?" on the basket bottom.

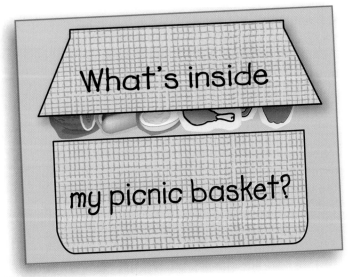

Spring and Summer

Fancy Sun Hat

Materials for one:

construction paper scraps
large white paper plate half
small white paper plate
craft materials, such as craft
   foam shapes and silk flowers

sentence strip
crayons
glue

Steps:

1. Color the back of the paper plate half (hat).
2. Glue the hat to the top of the small plate; then decorate the hat with craft materials.
3. Draw a face on the small paper plate. Add construction paper scraps for hair.
4. Label the sentence strip with "[Your Name] wears a sun hat." Glue the strip to the plate.

Barefoot in the Grass

Materials for one:

tub of water
copy of a poem card from
   page 137
dark green construction paper
light green construction
   paper scraps

tray
paper towels
skin-tone paint
scissors
glue

Setup:

Spread a layer of paint in the tray. Place the tray and the construction paper in front of a chair. Set a tub of water and paper towels next to the chair.

Steps:

1. Sit in the chair and dip your feet in the paint.
2. Press your feet on the paper to make footprints. Then dip your feet in the water and wash off the paint. Use the paper towels to dry them.
3. Cut the paper scraps into thin strips so they resemble grass; then glue the grass to the paper around the footprints.
4. Glue the poem to the paper.

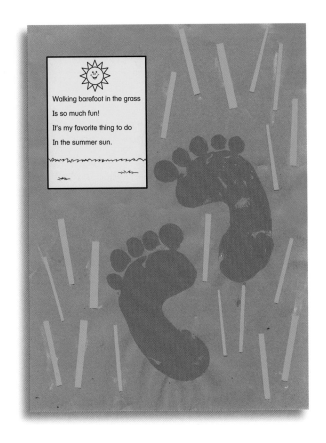

Spring and Summer

Shiny Yellow Sun

Materials for one:

white fingerpaint paper
small white paper plate
fork
yellow paint

paintbrush
gold glitter
glue

Setup:

Trace the paper plate onto the center of the paper.

Steps:

1. Paint the back of the plate; then sprinkle glitter on the wet paint.
2. Fingerpaint the paper around the outside of the circle.
3. To make the sun's rays, drag the fork's tines through the wet paint from the tracing toward each edge of the paper.
4. Glue the paper plate on the circle.

Natural Suncatcher

Materials for one:

4" to 6" twig
flat natural items, such as small leaves and grass
two 6" clear Con-Tact covering circles
1" light and dark green tissue paper squares
hole puncher
yarn

Steps:

1. Peel the backing off one circle and place it sticky-side up on a table.
2. Press tissue paper squares and natural items on the circle.
3. Peel the backing off the remaining circle; then press the sticky side of the circle on the decorated circle.
4. Use the hole puncher to make a hole near the edge of the suncatcher; then poke the twig through the hole.
5. Tie a length of yarn to the ends of the twig to make a hanger.

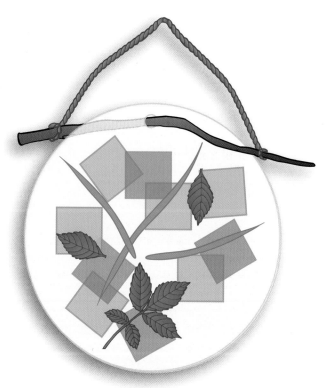

Fabulous Fireworks

Materials for one:
small evergreen branch
construction paper folded in half
shallow containers of red, white, and blue paint
glitter

Setup:
Cut the branch into three pieces. Place a branch next to each container of paint.

Steps:
1. Unfold the paper.
2. Press a branch in paint and then place it on the paper.
3. Fold the paper over the branch and then press on the paper.
4. Repeat the process with different branches and colors of paint.
5. Sprinkle glitter on the wet paint.

"Map-tastic" Headband

Materials for one:
used U.S. map   scissors
star-shaped cookie cutter   glue
3"-wide blue construction paper strip   stapler
shallow container of red paint

Steps:
1. Dip the cookie cutter in the paint and then press it on the map.
2. Repeat Step 1 several times. Let the paint dry.
3. Cut out the stars.
4. Glue the stars to the strip. *(Size the strip to fit the child's head and then staple it in place.)*

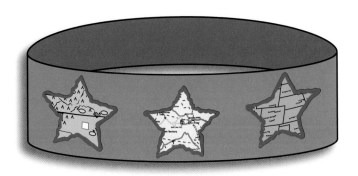

Spring and Summer

All-American Wreath

Materials for one:

photo of the child
white construction paper
large white paper plate
2 star-shaped sponges
shallow containers of red
    and blue paint

yarn
scissors
glue
hole puncher

Steps:

1. Dip a sponge in paint and then press it on the paper.
2. Repeat Step 1 several times with each paint color. Let the paint dry.
3. Cut out the stars.
4. Glue the stars around the rim of the plate.
5. Trim the photo, if needed, and glue it to the center of the plate.
6. Punch a hole in the top of the wreath and attach a yarn hanger. Write on the plate a patriotic statement, similar to the one shown, if desired (with help as needed).

Patriotic Pinwheel

Materials for one:

whisk
black construction paper
shallow container of glue
red, blue, and gold or silver glitter

Steps:

1. Dip the whisk in the glue and then press it on the paper.
2. Sprinkle glitter on the glue.
3. Repeat Steps 1 and 2 several more times.

Fancy Photo Easel

Materials for one:

photograph trimmed into a 3" square
3½" matboard or tagboard square
2 spring-style clothespins
3 jumbo craft sticks
markers
glue
glitter glue (optional)

Setup:

Glue the crafts sticks together as shown.

Steps:

1. Color the triangle and the clothespins.
2. Clip the clothespins to the triangle to make an easel.
3. Glue the photo to the matboard square.
4. Glue the matboard to the easel.
5. Decorate the easel with glitter glue, if desired.

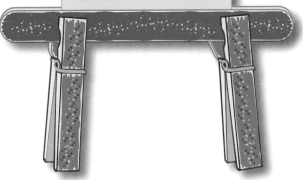

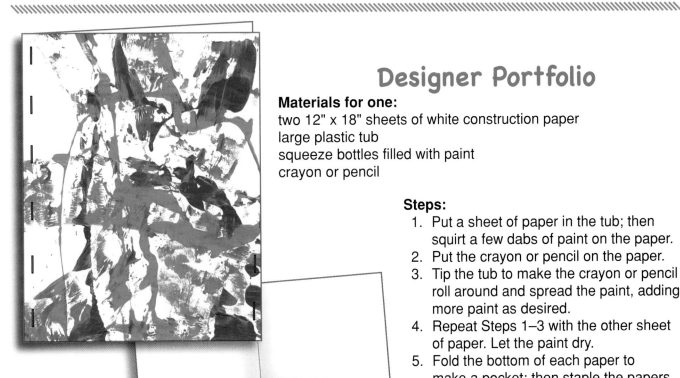

Designer Portfolio

Materials for one:

two 12" x 18" sheets of white construction paper
large plastic tub
squeeze bottles filled with paint
crayon or pencil

Steps:

1. Put a sheet of paper in the tub; then squirt a few dabs of paint on the paper.
2. Put the crayon or pencil on the paper.
3. Tip the tub to make the crayon or pencil roll around and spread the paint, adding more paint as desired.
4. Repeat Steps 1–3 with the other sheet of paper. Let the paint dry.
5. Fold the bottom of each paper to make a pocket; then staple the papers together along the left side and on the pocket edges.

Spring and Summer

Graduation Scroll

Materials for one:
2 small cardboard tubes
4½" x 18" white construction paper
large gold seal or star sticker
ribbon
glue
shallow container of paint
marker

Steps:
1. Glue the paper to the tubes to make a scroll.
2. Press your hand in the paint and then on the scroll. Let the paint and glue dry.
3. Put the gold seal or star sticker on the scroll.
4. Write your name on the scroll.
5. Thread the ribbon through the top tube and tie the ends together. *(Write the date and a special end-of-the-year sentiment on the scroll, if desired.)*

Congratulations

Nathan

You Graduated!

Butterfly Keepsake

Materials for one:
headshot photo of the child
6" x 9" colored construction paper
9" x 12" colored construction paper
9" x 12" light blue construction paper
2 thin black paper strips (antennae)

sequins
scissors
glue

Setup:
  Program the lower portion of the blue construction paper with the poem shown, replacing the name with the child's name. Set the paper aside.

Steps:
1. Trace your shoe on the small paper and cut out the tracing.
2. Trace your hands on the colored construction paper and cut out the tracings.
3. Glue the hand cutouts to the shoe cutout to make a butterfly.
4. Glue the photo, antennae, and sequins to the butterfly.
5. Glue the butterfly to the paper above the poem.

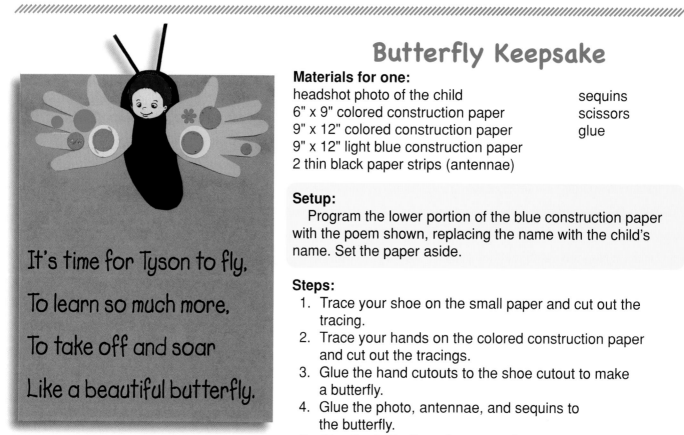

It's time for Tyson to fly,

To learn so much more,

To take off and soar

Like a beautiful butterfly.

Balloon Prints

Materials for one:
small balloons, slightly underinflated
construction paper
shallow container of different-colored paint
    for each balloon
markers

Steps:
1. Dip a balloon in paint and then press it lightly on the paper.
2. Repeat Step 1 with other balloons and colors of paint.
3. Draw a knot and string on each balloon print.

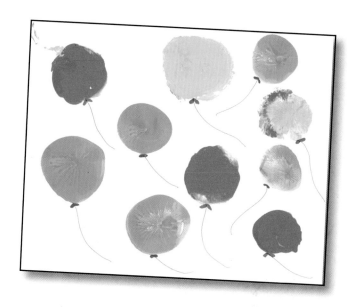

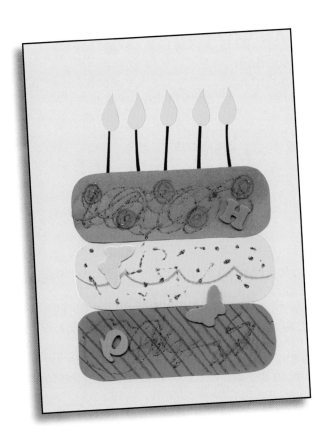

Layer Cake

Materials for one:

colorful construction paper strips trimmed as shown	self-adhesive craft foam shapes
construction paper	glitter pens
yellow construction paper flame cutouts	glue
	crayons

Steps:
1. Glue several strips to the construction paper so they resemble layers of a cake.
2. Use the foam shapes, glitter pens, and crayons to decorate the cake.
3. Draw candles to show how old you are.
4. Glue a flame to the top of each candle.

Anytime

Peekaboo Gift

Materials for one:

self-adhesive gift bow
gift wrap scraps
two 9" construction paper squares
used magazine
sticky note

scissors
glue
marker
stapler

Steps:

1. Cut gift wrap scraps and glue them to a square (gift); then attach the bow to the gift.
2. Write your name on the sticky note and attach it to the gift.
3. Cut pictures from the magazine of things you would like for your birthday; then glue them to the other square.
4. Place the gift atop the square and staple along the top edge. Lift the gift to reveal the desired items.

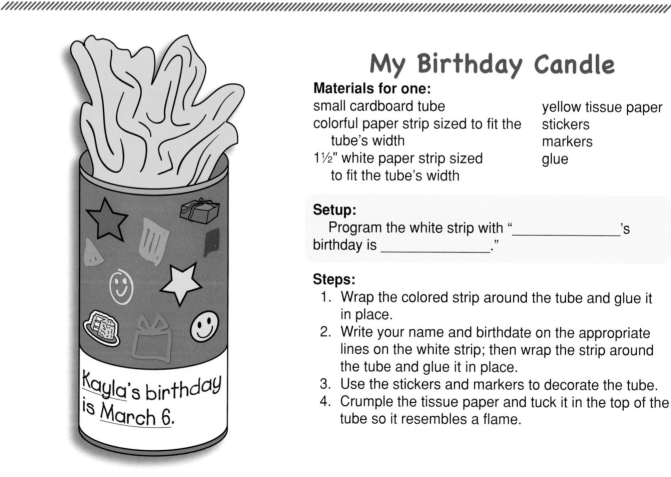

My Birthday Candle

Materials for one:

small cardboard tube
colorful paper strip sized to fit the
    tube's width
1½" white paper strip sized
    to fit the tube's width

yellow tissue paper
stickers
markers
glue

Setup:

Program the white strip with "_____'s birthday is _____."

Steps:

1. Wrap the colored strip around the tube and glue it in place.
2. Write your name and birthdate on the appropriate lines on the white strip; then wrap the strip around the tube and glue it in place.
3. Use the stickers and markers to decorate the tube.
4. Crumple the tissue paper and tuck it in the top of the tube so it resembles a flame.

Anytime

Birthday Balloon

Materials for one:
white tagboard balloon
shallow containers of tinted white corn syrup
curling ribbon
paintbrushes

Steps:
1. Paint the balloon any way you like, blending colors if desired. Let the balloon dry for several days.
2. Tie a length of ribbon to the balloon.

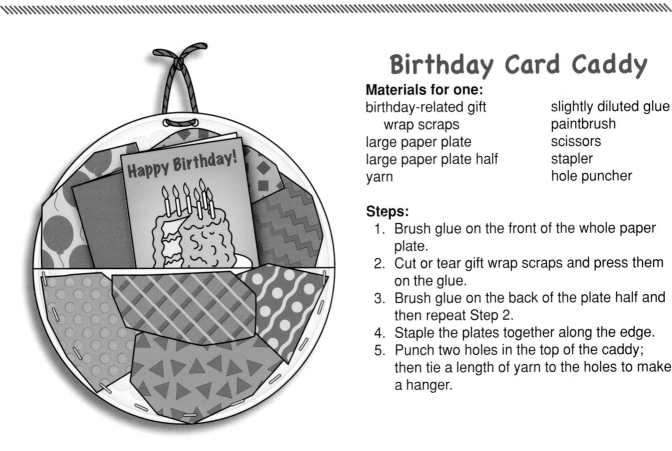

Birthday Card Caddy

Materials for one:

birthday-related gift wrap scraps	slightly diluted glue
large paper plate	paintbrush
large paper plate half	scissors
yarn	stapler
	hole puncher

Steps:
1. Brush glue on the front of the whole paper plate.
2. Cut or tear gift wrap scraps and press them on the glue.
3. Brush glue on the back of the plate half and then repeat Step 2.
4. Staple the plates together along the edge.
5. Punch two holes in the top of the caddy; then tie a length of yarn to the holes to make a hanger.

Anytime

Doctor's Kit

Materials for one:
adhesive bandage
3" x 4" black construction paper rectangle
two 2" x 4" red paper strips
9" x 12" sheet of black construction paper
jumbo craft stick
cotton ball
scissors
glue

Steps:
1. Fold the sheet of construction paper in half and round the corners (bag).
2. From the black rectangle, cut out a handle similar to the one shown and glue it to the back of the bag.
3. Glue the red strips to the front of the bag to make a cross.
4. Open the bag. Glue the craft stick and cotton ball inside and attach the bandage.

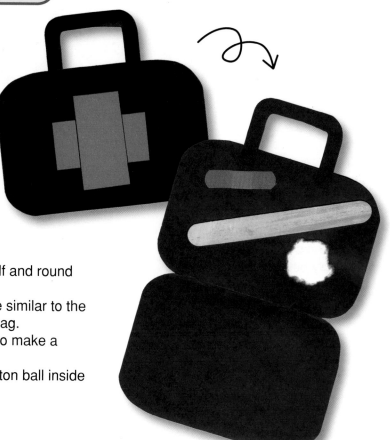

Police Officer's Hat

Materials for one:
construction paper police
 hat (pattern on page 139)
tagboard badge
 (pattern on page 139)
piece of aluminum foil larger
 than the badge

3" x 18" construction
 paper strip
crayons
glue
stapler

Steps:
1. Color the hat.
2. Place the badge cutout in the center of the aluminum foil and fold the aluminum foil over the sides of the badge until the badge is completely covered. Staple the badge to the center of the hat.
3. Glue the hat to the paper strip and allow the glue to dry. (Staple the strip to fit the child's head.)

Anytime

Building a House

Materials for one:
plastic toy hammers
construction paper house
shallows pans of paint

Setup:
   Place a hammer by each container of paint.

Steps:
1. Dip a hammer in a pan of paint.
2. Gently pound the hammer on the house.
3. Repeat Steps 1 and 2 with other hammers and colors of paint.

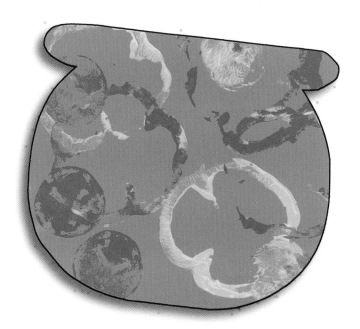

In the Chef's Pot

Materials for one:
variety of vegetables cut in half
large construction paper pot
shallow pans of paint

Setup:
   Place one or two cut vegetables by each paint color.

Steps:
1. Dip a vegetable in a container of paint.
2. Gently press the vegetable on the pot.
3. Repeat Steps 2 and 3 until the desired ingredients have been added to the pot.

Anytime

Library Collage

Materials for one:

small photo of child
children's book catalog
2¼" x 3½" white construction
   paper rectangle
construction paper
marker
scissors
glue stick

Setup:

Round the corners of the rectangle. Then program the rectangle with "Library Card" and a writing line as shown.

Steps:

1. Cut out pictures of your favorite books.
2. Glue the pictures to the paper.
3. Write your name on the library card.
4. Glue the photo to the library card.
5. Glue the library card to the paper.

Put Out the Flames

Materials for one:

10" x 13" piece of plastic wrap
2" x 6" green construction paper strip
9" x 12" white construction paper
blue construction paper scraps
red and yellow paint
glue

Steps:

1. Squirt red and yellow paint in the center of the white paper and cover the paper with plastic wrap.
2. Rub the plastic wrap to smooth the paint over the paper.
3. While the paint is still wet, remove the plastic wrap.
4. When the paint is dry, glue the green strip (hose) to the edge of the paper.
5. Tear the blue construction paper scraps and glue them to the end of the hose so they look like water.

Anytime

An Incredible Egg

Materials for one:
sheet of newspaper
masking tape
paint
paintbrush

Steps:
1. Tightly wad the newspaper into an oversize egg shape.
2. Tear long strips of masking tape and completely wrap the newspaper in the tape.
3. Paint the resulting egg as desired.

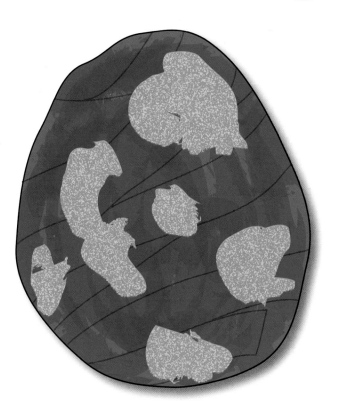

Fabulous Fossil

Materials for one:
6" x 9" Styrofoam piece
large construction paper rock cutout
craft stick
pencil
paint
paintbrush

Steps:
1. Use the craft stick and the pencil to draw dinosaur bones on the Styrofoam piece.
2. Paint the Styrofoam piece.
3. Press the Styrofoam piece on the rock cutout and use your hand to smooth over its surface.
4. Remove the Styrofoam piece.
5. Repeat Steps 2–4 one or two more times; then discard the Styrofoam piece.

Anytime

Textured Skin

Materials for one:
tagboard dinosaur cutout
3" x 12" green construction paper strip
9" x 12" blue construction paper
masking tape
scissors
glue
diluted light brown tempera paint
sponge piece
black permanent marker

Setup:
Tear tape into a variety of lengths and shapes. Attach one end of each piece to the edge of a table for easy removal.

Steps:
1. Fringe-cut the green paper strip and glue it to the bottom of the blue paper so it looks like grass.
2. Attach pieces of tape to the dinosaur until it is completely covered.
3. Sponge-paint the dinosaur.
4. When the paint is dry, use the black marker to draw details on the dinosaur.
5. Glue the dinosaur to the prepared blue paper as shown.

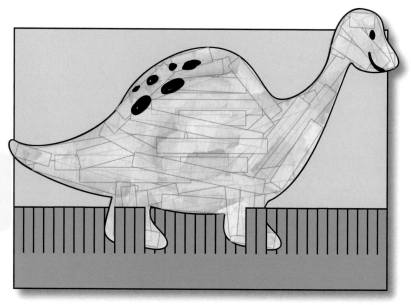

A Shapely Beast

Materials for one:
construction paper shapes in different colors and sizes
9" x 12" construction paper
glue
markers

Steps:
1. Arrange shapes on the construction paper sheet so they resemble a dinosaur.
2. Glue the shapes in place.
3. Use the markers to add details.

Anytime

Arts & Crafts for Favorite Themes • ©The Mailbox® Books • TEC61262

Dancing Dinosaurs

Materials for one:
plastic toy dinosaurs
construction paper
shallow pans of paint

Steps:

1. Dip a dinosaur's feet in the paint.
2. Press the dinosaur on the paper and "dance" it across the page.
3. Repeat Steps 1 and 2 with different dinosaurs and different colors of paint.

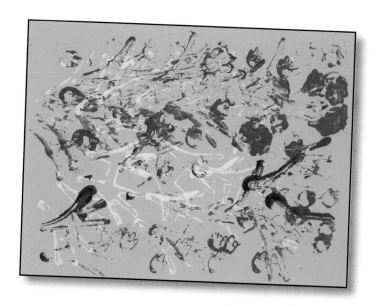

Ready to Hatch

Materials for one:
2 egg-half cutouts
construction paper scraps
paper cup
jumbo craft stick
scissors
markers
glue

Setup:
In the bottom of the cup, cut a slit slightly wider than the craft stick.

Steps:

1. Use the paper scraps and markers to decorate the top half of the craft stick to look like a baby dinosaur.
2. Glue each egg half to a different side of the paper cup.
3. Slide the craft stick through the slit so the dinosaur is hidden inside the cup.
4. Push the bottom of the craft stick up to make the dinosaur "hatch" from its egg.

Anytime

Fluffy Chick

Materials for one:
yellow construction paper oval
small orange construction paper triangle (beak)
construction paper scraps (for eyes)
resealable plastic bag
cotton balls
2 orange pipe cleaner halves
powdered yellow tempera paint
tape
glue

Steps:
1. Put the cotton balls and a small amount of paint in the plastic bag. Seal the bag and shake it until the cotton balls are coated.
2. To make a chick, glue the cotton balls on the oval. Glue two eyes and a beak atop the cotton balls.
3. Tape the pipe cleaners to the back of the chick and then bend the pipe cleaners to make feet.

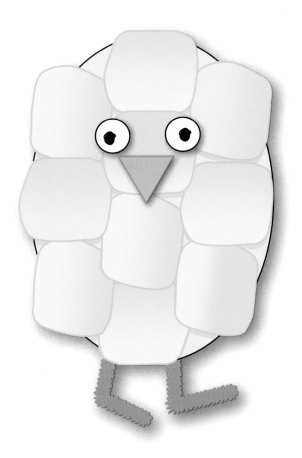

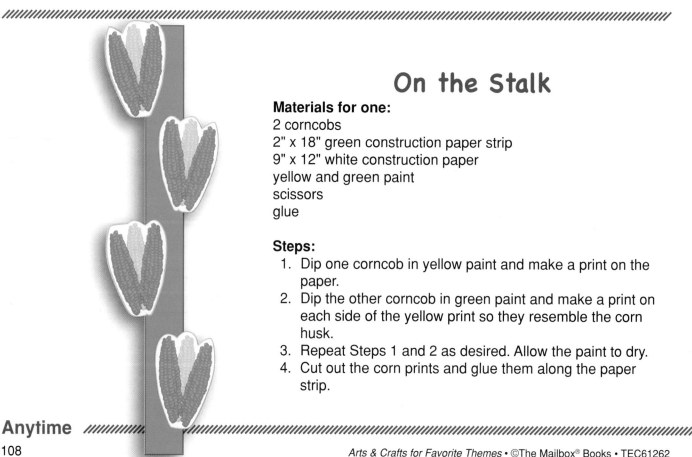

On the Stalk

Materials for one:
2 corncobs
2" x 18" green construction paper strip
9" x 12" white construction paper
yellow and green paint
scissors
glue

Steps:
1. Dip one corncob in yellow paint and make a print on the paper.
2. Dip the other corncob in green paint and make a print on each side of the yellow print so they resemble the corn husk.
3. Repeat Steps 1 and 2 as desired. Allow the paint to dry.
4. Cut out the corn prints and glue them along the paper strip.

Anytime

Happy Cow

Materials for one:

small milk carton
4 spring-style clothespins (legs)
construction paper scraps
length of twine
black paint

paintbrush
tape
scissors
glue
crayons

Setup:

Cut one side away from the milk carton. Then tape down the top of the carton.

Steps:

1. Paint the legs and allow the paint to dry.
2. Cover the carton with paper and add spot cutouts. Then clip the legs to the carton.
3. Cut out a cow-shaped head and use crayons to add details to it. Then glue the head to the front of the carton.
4. To add a tail, poke a small hole in the back of the carton and thread the twine through the hole. Secure the twine by tying a knot in each end.

Duck in the Pond

Materials for one:

2" yellow construction paper circle (head)
9" x 12" yellow construction paper
construction paper scraps

paper plate
crayons
scissors
glue

Steps:

1. Color the back of the paper plate yellow. Then fold the plate in half.
2. Use the paper scraps to add eyes and a beak to the circle. Then cut feet and legs from the paper scraps.
3. To make tail feathers, trace your hands on the yellow paper and then cut out the tracings.
4. Glue the head, legs, feet, and tail feathers to the paper plate as shown.

Anytime

Pig in the Mud

Materials for one:
nonmentholated shaving cream
pink copy of the pig pattern on page 140
9" x 12" construction paper
brown paint
glue
scissors

Setup:
Combine equal parts of shaving cream and glue. Then mix in a small amount of brown paint.

Steps:
1. Cut out the pig pattern and glue the cutout in the center of the paper.
2. Spread a large dollop of the shaving cream mixture below the pig so it looks like the pig is standing in mud.
3. Spread a few small blobs of the mixture on the pig.

Handsome Horse

Materials for one:

8" construction paper square	brown yarn pieces
four 1" x 8" construction paper strips	marker
	scissors
brown construction paper	glue

Steps:
1. Use the marker to trace your hand on the brown paper. Cut out the tracing.
2. Glue the cutout to the paper square with the fingers pointing down.
3. On the thumb, draw an eye and a mouth. Draw body details as desired.
4. Glue yarn pieces to the cutout so they resemble a horse's mane and tail.
5. Glue the paper strips to the square so they resemble a fence, trimming the strips as needed.

Anytime

Home, Sweet Home

Materials for one:
cardboard tube
large white construction
  paper house
flesh-tone paint
markers
crayons

Steps:
1. Use a marker to label the house as shown.
2. Dip one end of the cardboard tube in the paint and make a print for each member of your family. Allow the paint to dry.
3. Add a body and facial features to each print so it resembles a member of your family.

Family Flags

Materials for one:
9" x 12" white construction paper
large craft stick
pencil
paint
sponges
tape

Steps:
1. Draw lines to divide your paper into sections equal to the number of people in your family.
2. For each person in your family, sponge-paint a section in a color that reminds you of him or her. Allow the paint to dry.
3. Tape the craft stick to the back of your paper to make a flag.

Anytime

A Hug for My Family

Materials for one:
5" white construction paper circle (head)
8" construction paper square
two 2" x 18" construction paper strips
9" x 12" white construction paper
scissors
glue
crayons

Steps:
1. Color the head so it resembles your own.
2. Use scissors to round the top corners of the paper square. Then write "I love you this much!" on the square.
3. Trace your hands on the white paper and color the tracings with a flesh-tone crayon. Cut out the tracings.
4. To make arms, accordion-fold the paper strips and glue a hand cutout to one end of each paper strip.
5. Glue the head and the arms to the square as shown.

Family Puppets

Materials for one:
paper scraps	crayons
various lengths of	glue
hair-colored yarn	tape
small paper plates	scissors
craft sticks	

Steps:
1. Decorate each plate to resemble a family member.
2. Tape a craft stick to the back of each plate to make a puppet.

Anytime

Arts & Crafts for Favorite Themes • ©The Mailbox® Books • TEC61262

Faraway Constellation

Materials for one:

cardboard tube (telescope)
space-themed stickers
three 6" black tissue
　　paper squares

rubber band
pushpin
paint
paintbrush

Steps:

1. Paint the telescope and allow the paint to dry.
2. Decorate the telescope with stickers.
3. Place the tissue paper squares over one end of the telescope and use the rubber band to secure them.
4. To make a constellation pattern, use the pushpin to poke several holes in the tissue paper.
5. Hold the tube toward a light source and look through it to view the constellation.

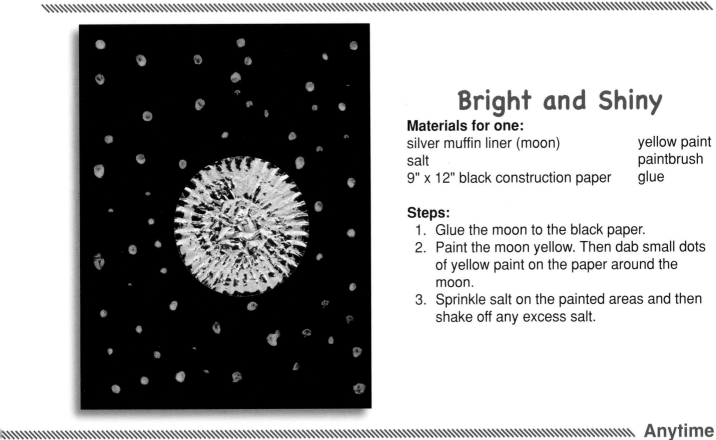

Bright and Shiny

Materials for one:

silver muffin liner (moon)
salt
9" x 12" black construction paper

yellow paint
paintbrush
glue

Steps:

1. Glue the moon to the black paper.
2. Paint the moon yellow. Then dab small dots of yellow paint on the paper around the moon.
3. Sprinkle salt on the painted areas and then shake off any excess salt.

Anytime

The Moon and Stars

Materials for one:

5" x 8" black and yellow
   construction paper rectangles
3" white construction paper square

hole puncher
scissors
glue

Steps:

1. Fold the black paper in half and then punch several holes in it.
2. Unfold the black paper and glue it atop the yellow paper.
3. Cut a moon from the white paper and glue it to the black paper.

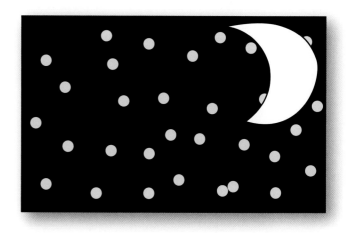

Rolled Planet

Materials for one:

golf ball
spoon
large box lid
8" tagboard circle tracer
9" construction paper square

yarn
scissors
containers of paint
hole puncher

Steps:

1. On the paper square, trace the circle and cut out the tracing (planet). Place the planet in the lid.
2. Use the spoon to dip the golf ball in a paint container and then place the ball in the lid.
3. Hold the sides of the lid and roll the golf ball around, making streaks across the planet. Let the paint dry.
4. Repeat Steps 2 and 3 using a different paint color.
5. Punch a hole near the top of the planet and add a loop of yarn for hanging.

Anytime

Bumpy Moon

Materials for one:

oatmeal
8" white construction
   paper circle (moon)
iridescent glitter

water
glue
white paint
paintbrush

Setup:

Mix the oatmeal, water, and glue together to make a paste.

Steps:

1. Put a dollop of the oatmeal paste on the moon. Use your hands to spread the paste over the entire surface of the moon. Allow the paste to dry.
2. Paint the moon.
3. Sprinkle glitter on the painted area and shake off any excess glitter.

Swirled Moon

Materials for one:

8" disposable cake pan
8" white construction paper circle (moon)
gold and silver paint
paintbrushes

Steps:

1. Place the cake pan upside down on the work surface. Then paint the bottom of the pan with gold and silver paint, being sure to swirl the colors together.
2. Lay the moon on the painted surface and rub your hands over the paper.
3. Remove the moon and set it aside to dry.

Anytime

Floating in Space

Materials for one:

X-acto knife (for teacher use)
copy of an astronaut pattern
   from page 141
12" x 18" white
   construction paper
craft stick

crayons
diluted black paint
paintbrush
scissors
tape

Steps:

1. On the white paper, draw a space scene.
2. Brush a layer of paint over the drawing. Allow the paint to dry. *(Then use the X-acto knife to cut a slit in the space scene.)*
3. Draw a face on the astronaut so it resembles yourself. Color and cut out the pattern.
4. Tape a craft stick to the back of the pattern to make a puppet.
5. Insert the puppet in the slit in the space scene.

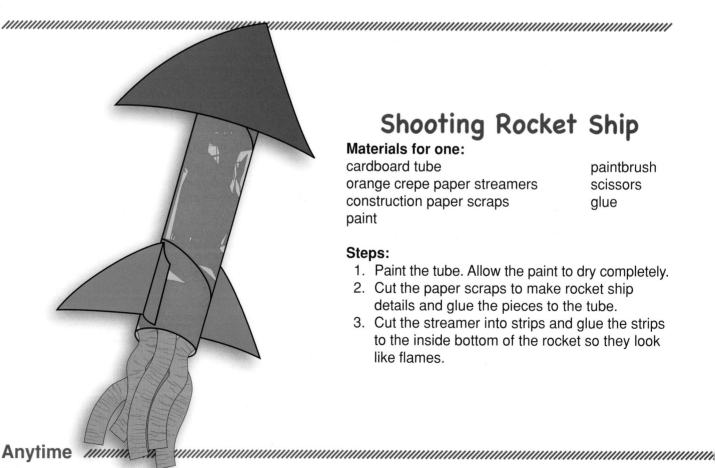

Shooting Rocket Ship

Materials for one:

cardboard tube
orange crepe paper streamers
construction paper scraps
paint

paintbrush
scissors
glue

Steps:

1. Paint the tube. Allow the paint to dry completely.
2. Cut the paper scraps to make rocket ship details and glue the pieces to the tube.
3. Cut the streamer into strips and glue the strips to the inside bottom of the rocket so they look like flames.

Anytime

Puppy Treats

Materials for one:

bone-shaped dog treats
large white construction
    paper jar
construction paper scrap
yarn

containers of different-
    colored paint
scissors
crayons
hole puncher

Steps:

1. Dip a dog treat in paint and then make a print on the jar.
2. Repeat Step 1 using the same or different colors of paint.
3. Use the paper scrap, scissors, and crayons to make a gift tag similar to the one shown.
4. Punch a hole near the top of the jar and in the tag. Then attach the tag to the jar with a length of yarn.

For Puppy

Elliot

In the House

Materials for one:

small milk carton (doghouse)
plastic toy dog
construction paper scrap
paint

paintbrushes
scissors
markers
glue

Setup:

Cut a doorway in one side of the milk carton.

Steps:

1. Paint the doghouse and allow the paint to dry.
2. Use the paper scrap, scissors, and markers to make a nameplate for the doghouse. Glue the nameplate over the doorway.
3. Place the toy dog inside the house.

Anytime

Kitty and Fishy

Materials for one:

construction paper fishbowl
3" orange construction paper circle
1" orange construction paper circle
2 orange construction paper triangles
construction paper scraps

crayons
scissors
glue

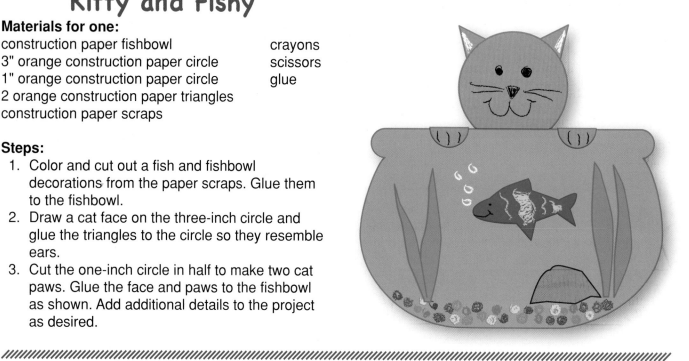

Steps:

1. Color and cut out a fish and fishbowl decorations from the paper scraps. Glue them to the fishbowl.
2. Draw a cat face on the three-inch circle and glue the triangles to the circle so they resemble ears.
3. Cut the one-inch circle in half to make two cat paws. Glue the face and paws to the fishbowl as shown. Add additional details to the project as desired.

Paper Plate Bunny

Materials for one:

two 1½" x 4" white construction
    paper strips
two 1" x 3½" pink construction
    paper strips
large paper plate
small paper plate
pink pom-pom

6 pipe cleaner
    halves
cotton ball
stapler
scissors
glue
crayons

Setup:

For each child, staple a small and large paper plate together as shown.

Steps:

1. To make the bunny's ears, trim the white and pink strips and then glue a pink strip to each white strip. Glue the ears to the top of the small paper plate (head).
2. Glue the pipe cleaners and pom-pom in the center of the head so they resemble a nose and whiskers.
3. Draw eyes and a mouth on the head.
4. Glue the cotton ball (tail) to the back of the bunny.

Anytime

Arts & Crafts for Favorite Themes • ©The Mailbox® Books • TEC61262

Furry Friend

Materials for one:

copy of the guinea pig
    pattern on page 142
9" x 12" construction paper
brown and orange paint

sponges
scissors
glue
marker

Steps:

1. Sponge-paint the guinea pig. Allow the paint to dry.
2. Cut out the guinea pig and glue it to the center of the construction paper.
3. Choose a name and write it below the guinea pig.

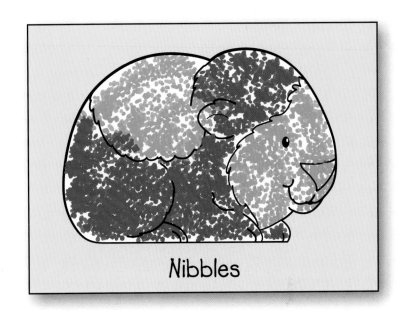

Nibbles

Terrific Turtle

Materials for one:

green construction
    paper scraps
green tissue
    paper squares
paper plate

glue
green paint
paintbrush
black marker

Setup:

Mix some glue in the paint.

Steps:

1. Brush the paint mixture on the back of the paper plate.
2. Place tissue paper squares on the plate to cover the painted area.
3. Tear the paper scraps to make the turtle's head, legs, and tail. Glue them to the paper plate as shown.
4. Draw a face on the turtle.

Anytime

Slithering Snake

Materials for one:

bottle caps
paper lunch bag
thin red paper strip
containers of different-
    colored paint

scissors
crayons
glue

Setup:
Keep the lunch bag folded and cut it to make a paper ring.

Steps:
1. Cut the paper ring to make a strip. Trim the ends so the strip resembles a snake.
2. Draw two eyes on one end of the snake. Then cut the red paper to make a tongue and glue it to the snake.
3. Dip a bottle cap in paint and make a print on the snake's body.
4. Repeat Step 3 using the same color of paint or a variety of colors.

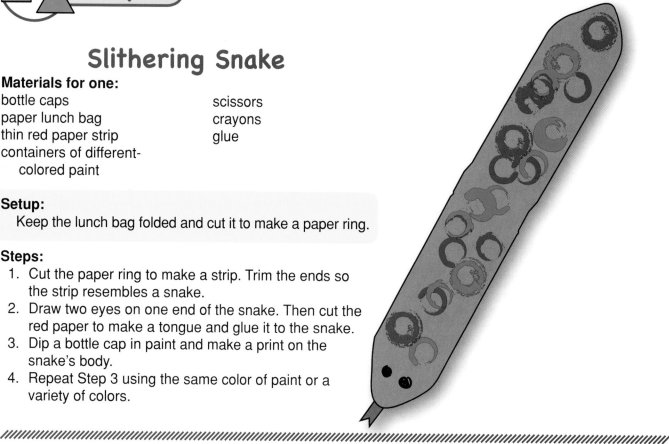

Shapely Lion

Materials for one:

five 1" x 4" yellow construction paper rectangles
5" x 8" yellow construction paper rectangle
5" yellow construction paper square
1" x 3" brown construction paper rectangle
two 1" black construction paper triangles
2 small black construction paper circles
12" x 18" construction paper
2" light and dark brown lengths of yarn
glue
crayons

Steps:
1. On the large paper, glue the square and large yellow rectangle to make the lion's head and body.
2. Add legs and a tail by gluing the remaining yellow rectangles to the paper.
3. Glue the brown rectangle, the triangles, and the circles to the lion as shown.
4. Use the crayons to add details to the lion.
5. Glue yarn around the lion's head to form a mane.

Anytime

Colorful Print Collage

Materials for one:

wipes

common-shaped objects—such as blocks, linking cubes, milk cartons with the tops cut off, and bottle caps—to make prints

9" x 12" construction paper

containers of paint

Setup:

Place the collection of objects near the containers of paint.

Steps:

1. Choose an object from the collection and dip it in paint. Then press the object on the paper to make a print. Make more prints with the object if desired.
2. Wipe the paint from the object and return it to the collection.
3. Repeat Steps 1 and 2 with other objects and colors of paint.

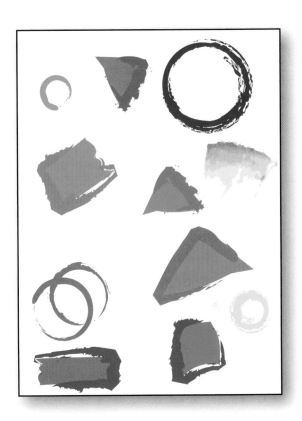

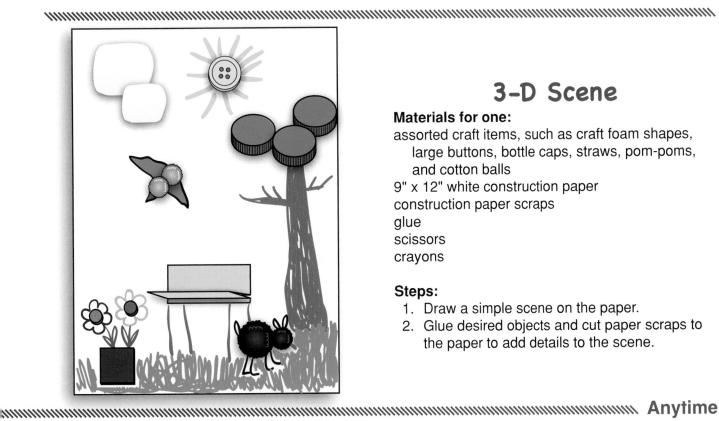

3-D Scene

Materials for one:

assorted craft items, such as craft foam shapes, large buttons, bottle caps, straws, pom-poms, and cotton balls

9" x 12" white construction paper

construction paper scraps

glue

scissors

crayons

Steps:

1. Draw a simple scene on the paper.
2. Glue desired objects and cut paper scraps to the paper to add details to the scene.

Anytime

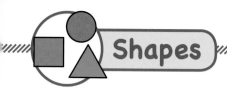

Family Portrait

Materials for one:
assorted construction paper circles, rectangles,
    triangles, and squares
9" x 12" white construction paper
glue
crayons
markers

Steps:

1. Decorate the edges of the white paper so it resembles a photo frame.
2. Glue one of each shape in the frame.
3. Draw facial features on each shape. Complete each shape person by drawing a body.

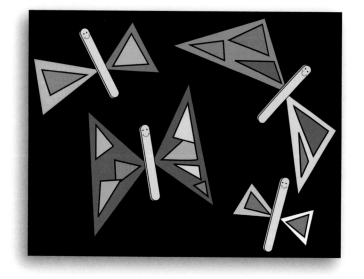

Beautiful Butterflies

Materials for one:
9" x 12" black construction
    paper
colorful paper scraps
miniature craft sticks

scissors
glue
fine-tip markers

Steps:

1. From the paper scraps, cut several triangles of various sizes.
2. Glue pairs of large triangles to the paper so they resemble butterfly wings.
3. Glue smaller triangles on the wings to make designs.
4. Glue a craft stick in the center of each pair of wings. If desired, draw a face on each craft stick.

Anytime

Shape Person

Materials for one:

four 1" x 9" paper strips   scissors
9" x 12" construction paper   glue
construction paper scraps   crayons
large shape tracer

Steps:

1. On the construction paper, trace the shape. Then cut out the tracing.
2. Accordian-fold the paper strips. Glue the strips to the shape cutout so they look like arms and legs.
3. Use the crayons and paper scraps to add details—such as a face, hands, and feet—to the shape person.

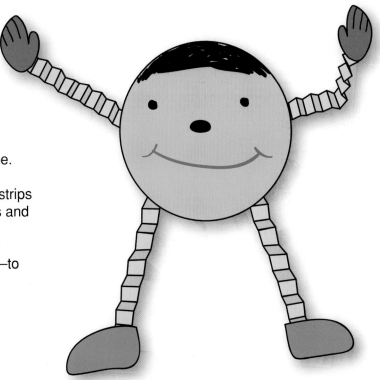

What Do You See?

Materials for one:

9" x 12" construction paper
large paper shape
glue
crayons

Steps:

1. Glue the shape to the center of the construction paper.
2. Draw details so the shape resembles a familiar object.
3. Draw additional details on the paper as desired.

Anytime

On the Road

Materials for one:
map page from a used atlas
vehicle- and sign-shaped sponges
containers of different-colored paint
black marker

Steps:

1. Dip the sponges in paint and make several prints on the atlas page. Allow the paint to dry.
2. Add words and arrows to the signs.

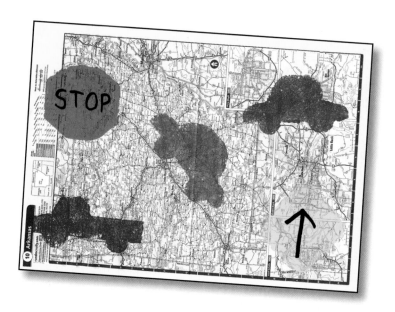

All Aboard!

Materials for one:

painter's tape   blocks
9" x 12" construction paper   paint
black paper scraps   scissors
sponge   glue
train engine–shaped sponge

Steps:

1. Place strips of painter's tape near the bottom of the paper so they resemble train tracks.
2. Sponge-paint between the tape pieces. Allow the paint to dry. Then carefully remove the tape.
3. Dip the engine-shaped sponge in paint and make a print on the paper.
4. Dip blocks in the paint and make prints behind the engine (train cars).
5. Cut wheels from the paper scraps and glue them below the engine and cars.

Anytime

Making Tracks

Materials for one:
baby wipes
assorted toy vehicles
9" x 12" construction paper
containers of different-colored paint

Steps:
1. Dip a vehicle in paint and then roll it across the paper.
2. When you are finished with the vehicle, clean it with a wipe.
3. Repeat Steps 1 and 2 using different vehicles and colors of paint.

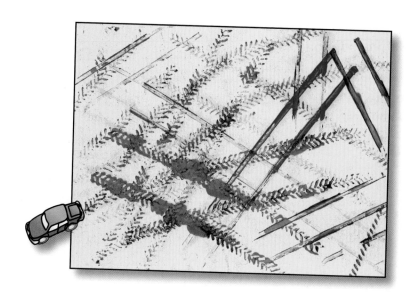

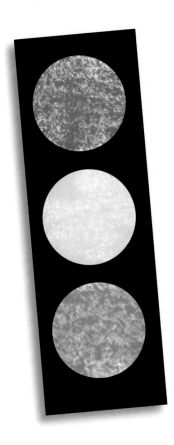

Traffic Light

Materials for one:
4" x 12" black construction paper rectangle
9" x 12" white construction paper
3" tagboard circle
red, yellow, and green paint
sponges
scissors
glue

Steps:
1. Sponge-paint a portion of the white paper using each color of paint. Allow the paint to dry.
2. Trace the circle in each painted portion of the paper. Cut out the tracings.
3. Glue the cutouts to the rectangle so it resembles a traffic light.

Anytime

Map It Out!

Materials for one:
building-shaped sponges
12" x 18" light-colored construction paper
containers of different-colored paint
markers

Steps:
1. On the paper, use the sponges and paint to make randomly placed buildings. Allow the paint to dry.
2. Draw roads and building details as desired.

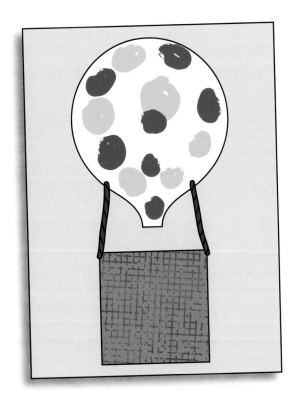

Fancy Hot-Air Balloon

Materials for one:
plastic canvas
white construction paper balloon
3" brown construction paper square
9" x 12" light blue construction paper
straw
2 lengths of yarn
slightly diluted paint
unwrapped brown crayon
glue

Steps:
1. Drip several drops of paint on the balloon.
2. Blow air through the straw to move the paint. Allow the paint to dry.
3. Place the paper square on the plastic canvas and then color the square.
4. Glue the square near the bottom of the light blue paper and the balloon near the top.
5. Glue the yarn between the balloon and square to connect them.

Anytime

Stop Sign

Materials for one:

white construction
  paper octagon
craft stick

white crayon
red and black markers
tape

Steps:

1. Use the white crayon to write "STOP" on the octagon.
2. Color the octagon with the red marker.
3. Color the craft stick with the black marker.
4. Tape the craft stick to the back of the octagon.

A Designer Boat

Materials for one:

triangle cut from patterned
  scrapbooking paper
paper cup
straw

play dough
crayons
markers
tape

Steps:

1. Use markers and crayons to decorate the cup.
2. Press a large ball of play dough in the cup.
3. Press one end of the straw into the play dough.
4. Tape the triangle to the straw so it looks like a sail.

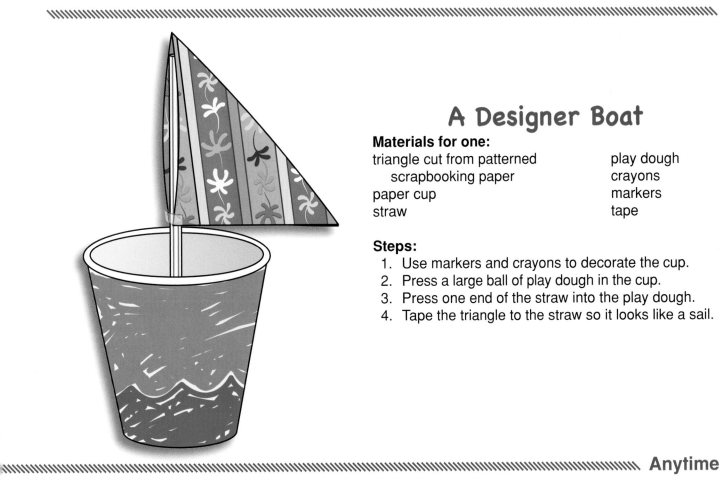

Anytime

Zookeeper's Vest

Materials for one:

animal sticker
large paper grocery bag
construction paper scraps

scissors
markers
glue

Setup:

Cut a line down the center of the front of the bag. Then cut a hole in the bottom of the bag for the child's neck and a hole in each side for the child's arms.

Steps:

1. Cut a nameplate and a badge from the paper scraps.
2. Write your name on the nameplate and glue it to a flap of the vest.
3. Write "Zookeeper" on the badge and put an animal sticker below the writing. Then glue the badge to the other flap of the vest.

Crazy Arms and Legs

Materials for one:

supply of 1" x 4" brown
   construction paper strips
light and dark brown
   construction paper scraps
paper lunch bag

newspaper
stapler
scissors
markers
glue

Steps:

1. Stuff the paper bag with newspaper. Then roll down the top of the bag and staple it.
2. Use the paper scraps, scissors, markers, and glue to make a monkey head. Glue it near the top of the bag.
3. To make each arm and leg, glue a paper strip to make a loop. Then link several more loops to it. Staple the arms and legs to the bag (with help as needed).

Anytime

Colorful Giraffe

Materials for one:
construction paper rectangles of various
   sizes and colors
9" x 12" construction paper
bingo daubers
glue
markers

Steps:
1. Arrange several rectangles on the construction paper so they resemble a giraffe. Glue them to the paper.
2. Use the markers to draw details on the giraffe.
3. Use the bingo daubers to add spots.

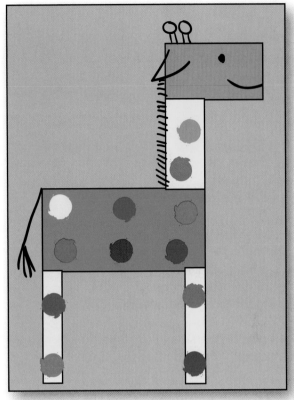

Invisible Stripes

Materials for one:
9" x 12" white construction paper
watercolors
paintbrush
black and white crayons

Steps:
1. On the paper, draw a zebra without stripes.
2. Use the white crayon to draw "invisible" stripes on the zebra.
3. Paint the zebra with the watercolors to make the stripes appear.

Anytime

Pretty Peacock

Materials for one:

small cardboard tube
five 1" x 6" white construction
  paper strips
2" x 6" white construction
  paper rectangle
watercolors

paintbrush
black paint
scissors
crayons
glue

Steps:

1. Paint the tube and the paper strips with watercolors.
2. Dip a finger in the black paint. Make a print at the top of each paper strip.
3. Cut a peacock's body from the paper rectangle. Color the body and add details.
4. Glue the body to one side of the tube.
5. Glue the strips to the opposite side of the tube so they resemble feathers.

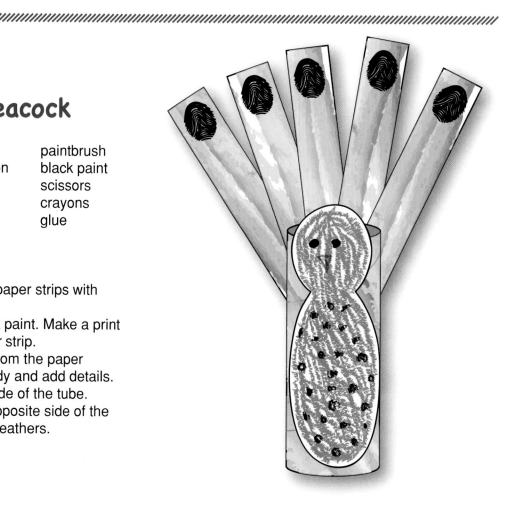

Fancy Flamingo

Materials for one:

9" x 12" white construction paper
pink paint
paintbrush
pink and black crayons

Steps:

1. Paint your hand and press it on the paper to make a print like the one shown. Allow the paint to dry.
2. Use the crayons to add a head and legs.

Anytime

TEC61262

Cornucopia Pattern
Use with "Cornucopia Collage" on page 24.

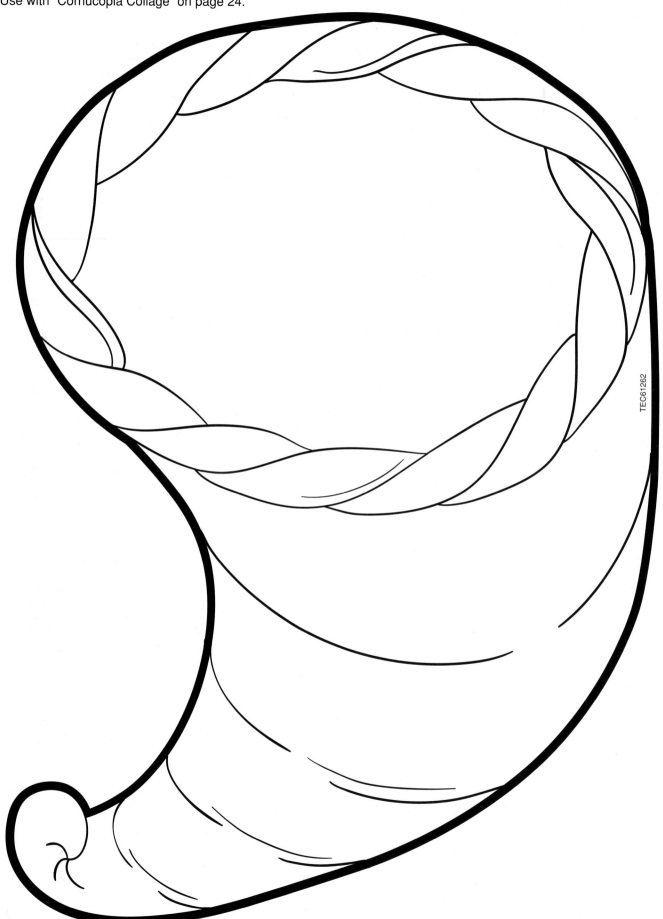

TEC61262

Arts & Crafts for Favorite Themes • ©The Mailbox® Books • TEC61262

TEC61262

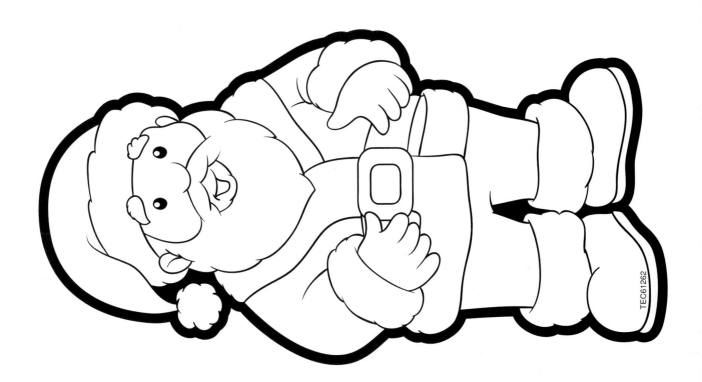

TEC61262

Groundhog Pattern

Use with "Groundhog's Shadow" on page 45.

TEC61262

TEC61262

TEC61262

Bunny Body Parts Patterns
Use with "Hop, Hop, Hop" on page 63.

TEC61262

Frog Pattern

Use with "Lots of Flies" on page 64.

TEC61262

Ice Cream Poem Cards

Use with "Oops!" on page 82.

Oops!	Oops!
My chocolate ice cream cone Started melting in the sun. Plop! I couldn't stop my cone From coming all undone. TEC61262	My chocolate ice cream cone Started melting in the sun. Plop! I couldn't stop my cone From coming all undone. TEC61262

Arts & Crafts for Favorite Themes • ©The Mailbox® Books • TEC61262

Walking barefoot in the grass

Is so much fun!

It's my favorite thing to do

In the summer sun.

TEC61262

Walking barefoot in the grass

Is so much fun!

It's my favorite thing to do

In the summer sun.

TEC61262

Walking barefoot in the grass

Is so much fun!

It's my favorite thing to do

In the summer sun.

TEC61262

Walking barefoot in the grass

Is so much fun!

It's my favorite thing to do

In the summer sun.

TEC61262

TEC61262

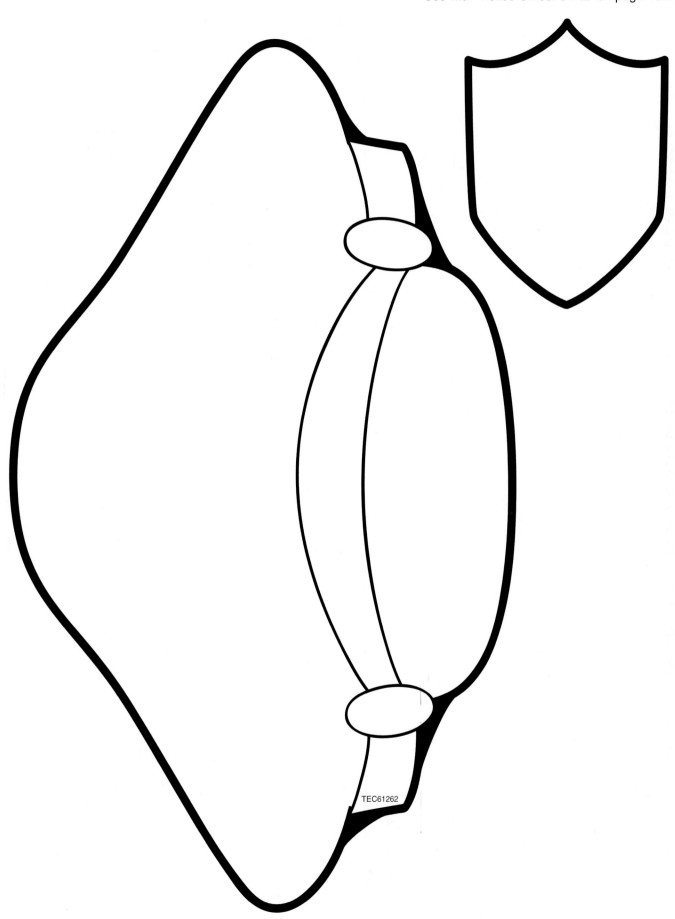

TEC61262

Pig Pattern

Use with "Pig in the Mud" on page 110.

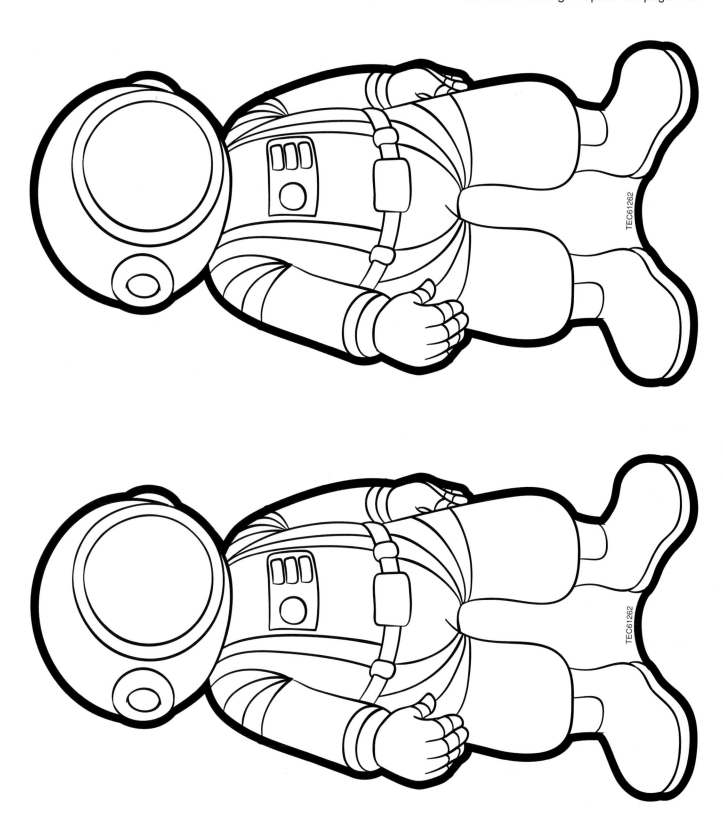

Guinea Pig Pattern
Use with "Furry Friend" on page 119.

TEC61262

142   *Arts & Crafts for Favorite Themes* • ©The Mailbox® Books • TEC61262

Arts & Crafts for Favorite Themes • ©The Mailbox® Books • TEC61262